What Kind of Past

The Story of a Balkan Sephardic Family

Author: Joe Youcha

A Publication of JewishGen, Inc.
Edmond J. Safra Plaza, 36 Battery Place, New York, NY 10280
646.494.5972 | info@JewishGen.org | www.jewishgen.org

An affiliate of New York's Museum of Jewish Heritage – A
Living Memorial to the Holocaust

Copyright © 2023 by Joe Youcha. All rights reserved.
First Printing: July 2023, Tammuz 5783

Author: Joe Youcha

Cover Design: Irv Osterer

This book may not be reproduced, in whole or in part, including illustrations in any form (beyond that copying permitted by Sections 107 and 108 of the U.S. Copyright Law and except by reviewers for public press), without written permission from the publisher.

JewishGen Inc. is not responsible for inaccuracies or omissions in the original work and makes no representations regarding the accuracy of this translation. Digital images of the original book's contents can be seen online at the New York Public Library website or the Yiddish Book Center website.

Printed in the United States of America by Lightning Source, Inc.

Library of Congress Control Number (LCCN): 2023941887

ISBN: 978-1-954176-79-9 (soft cover: 232 pages, alk. paper)

About JewishGen.org

JewishGen, an affiliate of the Museum of Jewish Heritage - A Living Memorial to the Holocaust, serves as the global home for Jewish genealogy.

Featuring unparalleled access to 30+ million records, it offers unique search tools, along with opportunities for researchers to connect with others who share similar interests. Award winning resources such as the Family Finder, Discussion Groups, and ViewMate, are relied upon by thousands each day.

In addition, JewishGen's extensive informational, educational and historical offerings, such as the Jewish Communities Database, Yizkor Book translations, InfoFiles, Family Tree of the Jewish People, and KehilaLinks, provide critical insights, first-hand accounts, and context about Jewish communal and familial life throughout the world.

Offered as a free resource, JewishGen.org has facilitated thousands of family connections and success stories, and is currently engaged in an intensive expansion effort that will bring many more records, tools, and resources to its collections.

Please visit https://www.jewishgen.org/ to learn more.

Executive Director: Avraham Groll

About JewishGen Press

JewishGen Press (formerly the Yizkor Books-in-Print Project) is the publishing division of JewishGen.org, and provides a venue for the publication of non-fiction books pertaining to Jewish genealogy, history, culture, and heritage.

In addition to the Yizkor Book category, publications in the Other Non-Fiction category include Shoah memoirs and research, genealogical research, collections of genealogical and historical materials, biographies, diaries and letters, studies of Jewish experience and cultural life in the past, academic theses, and other books of interest to the Jewish community.

Please visit https://www.jewishgen.org/Yizkor/ybip.html to learn more.

Director of JewishGen Press: Joel Alpert
Managing Editor - Jessica Feinstein
Publications Manager - Susan Rosin

What Kind of Past

A BALKAN SEPHARDIC FAMILY STORY

Joe Youcha

© 2023 Joseph Youcha

DEDICATION

To my dad, Isaac Zeke Youcha, who passed this heritage to me.
To my mom, Geraldine Shavelson Youcha, who
gave me the urge to write it down.

"To forget is to offend, and memory, when it is shared, abolishes this offence. If we want to share the beauty of the world, if we want to be in solidarity with its suffering, we need to learn how to remember together."

—Edouard Glissant

"Culture preserves the map and the records of past journeys so that no generation will permanently destroy the route."

—Wendell Berry

Map of the Southern Balkans after the Second Balkan War. (retrieved 11/15/2022, https://www.oldmapsonline.org/map/geoportost/BV042760552)

Preface

Traveling through family stories raises questions about which parts of heritage get carried forward, reclaimed, and taught. Not only pain gets passed down through families; joy and beauty do too. All this happens in the pages which follow.

Not many people know much about the country of North Macedonia in the southern Balkans. Fewer know the complicated history of this part of Europe, ruled for 500 years by a Muslim empire. My father's family comes from there. We're Sephardic Jews, Jews, expelled from Spain and Portugal around 1492 as part of the Inquisition. In the year when Columbus "discovered" America, the Ottoman Empire welcomed us. We experienced lives very different than those lived by the Jews ruled by Christians in the rest of Europe. Ours was an experience of mostly apathetic neglect rather than active persecution.

I jokingly say I'm the result of a "mixed marriage." My mom was Ashkenazi, the term for Jews who come from northern and eastern Europe. My mom's family immigrated from what's now Belarus. She was born in Rockland County, New York, about twenty-five miles north of New York City. She and I were born in the same hospital. (My two older sisters were born in "The City.") I grew up surrounded by my mother's history. In a soft voice, she told mostly nonjudgmental stories sympathetic to their subject or place. As the youngest, I spent a lot of time in the car alone with her driving through the areas where she grew up. Given her terrible sense of direction, I learned to navigate using landmarks from her 1930s childhood. Many of the houses, and most of the people, were gone by the 1970s, but I knew where they used to live and who they had been. I knew their stories, and I knew my mom's family's stories. The characters in my mom's family were fairly well-rounded even though they may have been dead for over 50 years. I knew their good sides, as well as many of their faults. I'm sure part of this was due to my mom being a journalist. She knew how to tell a story and develop characters.

While we lived near my mom's hometown, my father's culture dominated the food and gatherings in our house. I grew up calling myself Sephardic. Yet, I really didn't know my father's family stories the same way as I knew my mom's. I heard about the crazy aunt and the communist cousins. They were caricatures rather than characters, but they were just as much my ancestors. Their experiences flowed through to my children, just as my mom's, but the flow felt confused and jumbled. There were rapids in that river. Researching my father's side of the family helped smooth out some of those inter-generational disruptions.

I didn't start the research into my family. That was done by my cousin, Linda, who married my father's nephew, Victor. Even though she isn't a blood relative, Linda dug into our families' pasts and relentlessly pursued many document trails. Sadly, right before I started my work, Linda suffered a disabling stroke. Her daughter, Emily, has carried the research forward. Rarely have I found a resource that Emily or Linda didn't know about or hadn't thought of pursuing. I've been lucky with my timing. A remarkable set of circumstances and coincidences came together, enabling me to tell this story.

Like my father I also married a smart, supportive, and wonderful Ashkenazi woman, Jessica Kaplan. Our children Emma and Zack are only one quarter Sephardic. Largely due to the influence of my father and his fascination with the story of Sephardic Jewry, they too identify most strongly with that culture.

My father passed his interest in history to me. Even though I've spent my working life as a carpenter, wooden boat builder, educator, and nonprofit executive, my college degree is in history. My dad is interested in the grand narrative. "We thrived in Spain, were brutally expelled during the Inquisition, welcomed into the Ottoman Empire, and then, in our case, came to prosperity in America."

I'm now 60 years old; my dad is 95. I've heard my whole life about how we're just links in the chain of an historical continuum. Sometimes I rebelled against that idea. Doing this research made me realize that I'm more interested in the people. What do the other individual links of that chain look like? I'm not so curious about the greater spans.

In this book, I want to take some of the techniques I learned from my mom and round out the caricatures of my father's family into more nuanced characters, especially my grandfather, Victor, and his father, Jacob. Four years of research bookended by two family trips to Macedonia in 2018 and 2022 enabled me to be able to tell this part of my family story. It's not the complete story. It can't be. Family research is a continuing process. The more we learn, the more there is to learn.

Before we start digging into this story, I want to give a very brief history of the Balkans and how the Jews fit in.

Edward Lear Painting of Jewish Monastir 1848. (Courtesy of Houghton Library, Harvard University)

Above: Postcard View of Monastir.

Kal Aragon Synagogue by the Manaki Brothers. (Courtesy of the National Archives, Bitola)

Southern Balkan Jewish History— In a Nutshell

Monastir

Bitola, North Macedonia, the town my family still calls Monastir, sits on the Pelagonia plain surrounded by three mountain ranges, just above the current border with Greece and along the road the Romans called *Via Egnatia*. A mosaic from a synagogue floor in the nearby town Stobi indicates that Jews lived in the area by 200 AD. The dominant culture of Jewish Monastir started when King Ferdinand and Queen Isabella followed the advice of the Grand Inquisitor, Father Tomas de Torquemada, and expelled the Jews from Spain in 1492. The Sultan welcomed over 40,000 Sephardic Jews who brought technology and trade. The first graves in the Jewish cemetery in Monastir date from 1497, only two years after the expulsion. Two major synagogues established in town, Kal Aragon and Kal Portugal, reflect the original lands of their congregations, the kingdoms of Aragon and Portugal. ("Kal" means "community" in Hebrew.)

By about 1400, the Ottoman Turks ruled most of the Balkan Peninsula. For Christians and Jews, their rule was generally benign. The Pact of Umar which evolved within Islam over the previous centuries made us "Dhimmi," or "peoples of the book." We paid more taxes, lived with fewer rights, but didn't serve in the military. For Jews, it was a good deal, especially when compared to the ghettos and deadly pogroms of Christian Europe.

A frontier town, Monastir stood on the border of the Ottoman Empire and Europe, at times the greatest of enemies and at other times the greatest of trading partners. Monastir's location made it the "City of Consuls," where representatives of foreign governments helped conduct business. The town's position also made it a Turkish military headquarters with barracks and a training academy.

The Eastern Question

Ottoman Macedonia was claimed by many cultures. This became a problem in the nineteenth century with the rise of nationalism. Reading the history of the area, one gets the strong impression that the great powers of Europe used the Christian populations of the Balkans as pawns. For different strategic reasons, Russia, Austria-Hungary, Germany, and England all wanted a piece of the Balkan pie—either for their own direct benefit, or to keep their rivals in check.

Their policies found fertile ground for fomenting insurrection. Christians under Ottomans rule felt oppressed compared to their coreligionists in neighboring countries. For example, in Ottoman territories, the height of churches was limited, resulting in many of the old churches we see today being mostly underground. Pieces of the Ottoman Balkans were broken off into small Christian-dominated nations, starting with the Greek War of Independence from 1821 to 1829, the Serbian Revolution in the first decades of the nineteenth century, and through the Russian-Turkish War of 1878. This was not good for the Jews. One of the last European regions left under Ottoman rule was "Macedonia." Ottoman Macedonia included parts of current northern Greece, the Republic of North Macedonia, Albania, Bulgaria, and Turkey. The effects of religious nationalism reverberated in the region. Lots of peoples felt they claimed an historic right to this land. They still do.

On our first trip to the area in 2018, we learned that, upon independence in 1878, the Bulgarians tore down over seventy percent of the mosques in their country. Bulgarian textbooks still refer to Ottoman rule as a time of enslavement. The latest Bulgarian expulsion of Muslims happened in the 1980s when Muslims fled to avoid taking Christian names. Many, many left.

The Illinden Uprising

In 1903, the Turks ruthlessly crushed Macedonian revolutionaries trying to achieve an independent, united Macedonia. By that time, the Greeks, Bulgarians, and Serbs had all carved out their own countries. The Macedonians wanted independence too and certainly didn't want to trade the Turks for a different master. The rebelling nationalists fought hard against the Turks. Their battle originated the word "terrorist" in the English language. For ten days, Macedonian revolutionaries in a few villages even declared an independent state. This event now serves as part of North Macedonia's national creation story. Although centered in Salonica (now, Thessaloniki, Greece), the revolt spread throughout countryside villages and into other Macedonian cities. During that period, Monastir became the "City of Bombs." It was a brutal time that simmered for many, many months before it exploded on August 3rd, 1903—Elijah's, or Illinden's, Day. The Turks crushed the revolt.

Young Turk Revolution

The early 1900s saw the Ottoman Empire ruled by a reactionary Sultan. In 1908, a group of young military officers, many trained at Monastir's military academy, revolted. These "Young Turks" tried to implement a more Western, less corrupt, constitutional monarchy. People became citizens of the Empire, rather than just subjects of the Sultan. For the Jews, amongst other things, this meant that military service became mandatory. The Young Turk revolution was warmly welcomed for all its potential, and soon despised for its failures.

The First and Second Balkan Wars

In 1912, Greece, Bulgaria, Montenegro, and Serbia invaded the European portion of the Ottoman Empire in order to carve it up amongst themselves. They were wildly successful. Monastir was on the front lines, the scene of a three-day battle between the Turks and Serbs. If not stopped by the Western powers, the Bulgarians would likely have taken Constantinople, the capital of the Ottoman Empire. The Serbians conquered Monastir, which became part of their country even though a prewar agreement gave it to Bulgaria. Over 500 years of Ottoman rule ended, and the victors each took their piece of Macedonia. Families were separated. Many businesses and trading arrangements were no longer legal, or practical—especially since Salonica, Monastir's big sister, was now Thessaloniki and part of Greece. The Serbs also changed Monastir's name to Bitola.

At the peace settlement table, the European powers didn't let the Bulgarians keep their conquered land, while the Serbs were given more of Macedonia than the Bulgarians thought they deserved. This led to the Second Balkan War in 1913, when Bulgaria attacked its former allies. It did not go well for the Bulgarians, especially when the Turks attacked and took back much of their former territory in Thrace, the plain to the east of Monastir and Salonica. This whole back and forth left injured national pride in all the countries, the ramifications of which were felt through World War One and World War Two.

Jewish Emigration

Many Jews left this area starting in the early 1900s. The peak of emigration was just before, during, and right after, the Balkan Wars. People left for South and Central America, as well as Europe and Palestine. Most, like my family, went to the United States.

World War One

World War One destroyed Bitola. Bulgaria and its allies, Germany and Austria-Hungary, captured the town from the Serbs in 1914. In 1915, the Allied troops, mainly French and Serbian, recaptured the town. The Bulgarians and Germans retreated into the mountains and set up their artillery. For 22 months, until September 1918, they constantly shelled and bombed the town. At some point the French decided to start using poison gas shells. The Bulgarians and Germans responded in kind and added incendiary shells. The town was almost totally destroyed. It seems everybody who could leave, did.

Inter War Period

Once the war ended, people started to return to what was left of Bitola. Many of the returning Jews tried to continue their lives in the town.

The American Jewish community from Monastir/Bitola sent clothes and money to their brethren back home. Many Bitolan Jews emigrated. Until the US instituted strict immigration laws in 1924, most tried to come to America. After 1924, when coming to the US was almost impossible, a strong Zionist movement in the town sent people to British-occupied Palestine.

World War Two and the Holocaust

Now part of the Kingdom of Yugoslavia established after World War One, Bitola limped along through the worldwide depression and the start of World War Two. In 1941, Nazi Germany and its Bulgarian ally invaded Yugoslavia and occupied Bitola. These were the darkest days for the Jewish community. The Bulgarian occupiers severely restricted their activities and movement while stealing all their property through "taxes" and the forced deposit of money into Bulgarian National Bank accounts. Naturally, the bank soon froze and confiscated the money. With the deportation of over 3,200 Jews on March 11, 1943, and their subsequent murder at Treblinka, the German death camp in Poland, the Jewish community in Monastir ended.

Salonica

It's hard to talk about Monastir without talking about its big sister, Salonica. Salonica was closely linked to Monastir by people, culture, and commerce. A railway connecting the towns was built in 1894. Monastir's prosperity depended upon its connection with the Aegean port city.

Called by the Jews "la madre de Israel" (the mother of Israel), along with Constantinople, Salonica was a center of Judaism and Jewish learning in the Ottoman Empire. The empire's second largest port, it was the economic hub of Ottoman Macedonia and dominated by its Jewish population, which at times was a majority. The main Jewish neighborhood adjoined the port. The Jews controlled the transport of goods to, and from, the ships. Jewish influence even made the city's official day of rest Saturday, the Hebrew sabbath. In 1903, the city served as the focal point of the Illinden Uprising.

Monastir almost always felt the effects of what happened in Salonica. The Jews from Salonica regarded the Jews from Monastir (Monastirlis) as their hillbilly cousins. And, cousins they were. When my family and I visited Salonica (now Thessaloniki) in 2018, we saw that the only synagogue to survive the Nazis was built by, and for, the Monastirlis who came to Salonica after the First World War.

In 1917, while the Jews from Monastir fled the shelling of the First World War, Salonica suffered a catastrophic fire that destroyed the port and the surrounding Jewish neighborhood. Yet, the Jews from Monastir still came. It gives an idea about how bad it must have been in my grandfather's hometown.

Salonica suffered, like Monastir, from the breakup of the Ottoman Empire. The fire, the wars, and the Greek takeover of the city all led to major Jewish emigration.

Salonica's Port, circa 1913. Auguste Léon for Albert Kahn, Albert-Kahn Departmental Museum, Department of Hauts-de-Seine, France.

Bitola
North Macedonia
June 2018

Our tour guide, Rante, called to the young woman in the garden, asking in Macedonian if she knew how to find the street. When they occupied the town during World War Two, the Bulgarians named it "Lozengrad." She shook her head and asked her father-in-law who shrugged apologetically. With only an hour to walk through the old Jewish neighborhood of Bitola, we made our excuses to the woman. "Wait, my husband will know." Over our protests, a few minutes later a man wearing a tracksuit and sandals came out of the house. He looked to be about forty with an earring and a hip, scruffy beard. It was a Monday, and he was taking the day off from his work as a national archivist.

Offhand, he couldn't identify the street but knew there was a book that cross-referenced the street names of the town as it changed from the rule of the Kingdom of Yugoslavia, to the Bulgarian occupation in World War Two, to Tito's Republic of Yugoslavia. While it was great that such a book existed, we soon needed to be back on the bus continuing our Sephardic Jewish Heritage tour of the Balkans. The archivist continued, "And you know, two weeks ago I uploaded that book to Facebook."

He took out his phone and a few minutes later, after apologizing for the slow connectivity, directed us to a curvy street. That was the one. We thought we were on our way to find the house of my great grandfather. We now had translated the address of Jacob Samuel Ishach, as it was listed in the German deportation papers of March 11, 1943, into the present day.

Our 2018 Trip

I was in Macedonia during June 2018, because my wife, Jessica, decided that she wanted to take a Sephardic heritage tour of the Balkans. An Ashkenazi Jew, Jessica had no ties to Sephardic Jews before marrying me. Jessica is, however, an historian and researcher. She, Emma (our eldest), and Jessica's sister, Karen, were going. If I wanted to come, I was welcome. I think it was actually Emma's interest in Judaism, our Sephardic heritage, and its language, Ladino, that provided the major spark for my participation. Truly, I never had a great desire to go back to my grandfather's country. I imagined nothing was left and that the family knew all there was to know. I liked history, but "finding my roots" wasn't my thing. Still, the trip sounded interesting. Besides, I didn't want to be left behind.

Led by Joseph Benatov, a lovely, very knowledgeable Bulgarian Jew who teaches at the University of Pennsylvania, our ten-day trip covered Bulgaria, Macedonia, and northern Greece. Bojan Rantasa, "Rante," was our local Macedonian tour guide. We had parts of three days in Macedonia, but only a morning in Monastir/Bitola.

We started the Macedonian leg of our trip in Skopje, the capital of North Macedonia, or, at the time, more correctly, The Former Yugoslav Republic of Macedonia. We first stopped at the new Holocaust Memorial Museum, funded by the Macedonian government's restitution to the remaining Macedonian Jewish community. Located prominently, right in the center of town, every school child in Macedonia must visit and be exposed to its story. They need to learn how a culture that flourished in their country for over 400 years was quickly destroyed by irrational hatred. After driving through the country and seeing the opposing crosses and mosques in village after village, this work obviously needs to be done.

On the ground floor of the museum are horizontal scrolls containing the names of the over 11,000 people from Skopje, Bitola, and Stip the Bulgarians and Germans deported and murdered in 1943. Behind the scrolls are replica tombstones from the cemetery in Bitola. At their center sits an urn with ashes from Treblinka. Pictures of some of the people murdered dominate the exhibit space. Only two percent of the Jews from Bitola survived the Second World War. Many young people joined the local resistance fighters, called partisans, and battled the Germans and

Bulgarians in the countryside. Some survived. Several Jewish doctors and pharmacists were spared because the Bulgarians needed their services. No one came back from Treblinka.

Left: Isaac Alboher in 1942 for the Bulgarian Police Registry. (Courtesy of United States Holocaust Memorial Museum) Right: Uncle Jack and Grandma in New York during World War Two. (Youcha family photo)

Very efficient in their work, the occupying Bulgarians compiled a registry of all the Jews: last name, first name, father's name, head of household, occupation, and address. They even took family photographs and pasted them into the book to prevent Jews from hiding. For those who didn't have pictures, the occupiers commissioned a local photographer to take portraits. The pictures in the museum are taken from the Bulgarian registry. One young man's picture jumped out at us. He bears a striking resemblance to a photo we have of my father's brother, my Uncle Jack. Taken during World War Two, Jack is in his Coast Guard uniform. The pictures were taken around the same time, in 1942. The two young men could have been brothers.

Even though it was officially closed for the installation of a new exhibit, the curator of the museum, Maja, gave us a tour. When she found out that Emma and I were Monastirlis (the descendants of people originally from Monastir), she got very excited, took me up to her offices and gave me copies of six books written in English documenting the Macedonian Jews' fate. Maja also gave me her card, offering her help. I told her that the research of my cousins, Linda and Emily, led them to think the family name might be some form of "Ishach." There weren't any "Youchas" on the German deportation lists, but Linda corresponded with people in Israel who connected Ishach to names similar to Youcha. One of the books Maja gave me confirmed that idea. We knew my great grandfather's first name was Jacob, and he was born around 1860. We also knew that he remarried after my great grandmother, Anna, died. We knew nothing about his second family.

When we parted, Maja said she'd check the records and look for a Jacob Ishach, but that it probably wouldn't be before we visited Bitola two days later. She said that Mima, the woman running the cemetery restoration project in Bitola, would be the best person to help.

As we left the museum, an older man from our trip, Jerry, told me very directly that if I could find where my great grandfather lived with his second family, I absolutely should. Coming into the trip, I wanted to let things come to me. I didn't do any extra preparatory research. I just carried the family knowledge and stories in my head. And now, unexpected facts and resources started popping up all around me.

Finding Jacob Samuel Ishach

The next day we were in Ohrid, a beautiful, historic lakeside town. After a dinner beside the water, we went back to the hotel. We were only going to have the next morning in Bitola. Jerry's words about finding my great grandfather and his address kept coming back to me.

The Internet can be a terrific thing. Using my phone, I found the German copy of the 1943 Bulgarian deportation list for Bitolan Jews with over 250 people having some form of Ishach as their last name. I thought I found our great grandfather and his second family on line 1130. He was Jacob Samuel Ishach, born on January 4, 1861. His middle name told us his father's name, Samuel. He was married to Sihul, born March 4, 1859. They lived in their daughter-in-law Rahel's house, 13 Lozengrad.

At three o'clock in the morning, I realized the street's name changed between 1942 and 2018. Google Maps did not show a Lozengrad Street. I looked for an old map of Bitola online and found none. In the first of this story's many coincidences, Lozengrad is the Bulgarian name for the town Kirklareli/Kir Kilisse in Turkish Thrace. It was the scene of a great Bulgaria victory over the Ottomans in the first Balkan war. It was also my grandmother's hometown. I didn't get a lot of sleep that night.

The next morning, before heading to Bitola, I cornered our guides, Joseph and Rante, at breakfast with the address I'd found and the need for a relevant map. Joseph believed that the woman leading the restoration of Bitola's Jewish cemetery our best bet. Rante added a thought. "We need to find an old postman." The same street likely changed names many times during the last one hundred years. Rante and his network of friends found an old mailman by the time we reached Bitola. This man remembered Lozengrad as being off one of two streets in what was left of an old Jewish neighborhood. We'd be able to look while the rest of the group went to lunch. First, we had to visit the cemetery and then see a Holocaust memorial dedicated to the town's Jewish population.

The largest surviving Jewish cemetery in Macedonia, and one of the largest in the Balkans, Bitola's cemetery sits on the side of a hill, mostly neglected since the end of World War Two. Recently, a project funded in part by the same restitution money as the Holocaust Museum in Skopje, restored the grounds, and scanned many of the tombstones which are gradually being translated. We walked amongst the graves trying to read the inscriptions on the long, horizontal stones. Unlike most vertical tombstones, these have room to really tell stories about the person they memorialize, many have illustrations and symbols that add context to the person's life. Supposedly, the earliest grave dates from 1497. The latest we found was marked 1942. Thousands of graves commemorate the lives of the Jews who lived in this community for the intervening 445 years. Our weak Hebrew didn't find any stones with the name Ishach.

Towards the end of our time there, Emma, Jessica, Karen, and I wandered away from the group with our tour mate Yaakov Bernstein. Yaakov led us in the Sephardic Kaddish, or mourner's prayer. After we scooted back to the rest of the group, another tour mate asked if we could all say Kaddish together. The whole group of twenty-five joined in. It was tremendously moving. Four hundred years of my ancestors are likely buried there, on the slope of that hill.

Back on the bus, we went to see the Bitolan Holocaust memorial in front of a hospital built on ground that was much of the oldest Jewish neighborhood. When the rest of the group went to lunch with Joseph, Rante took our family aside into the remaining streets, and soon we were standing in front of the archivist's garden, asking his wife if she knew the location of Lozengrad Street. Following her husband's directions, we found the empty lot where the house would have been. I didn't realize I was taking the first steps on a journey of coincidence and connections that would change how my family saw itself.

Jacob Samuel, or Jacob Isaac?

Once we left Macedonia for Greece, I sat down at my phone and emailed my family an update about everything we were "discovering." The next day I felt deluged by emails from my cousin Emily. Before we left on the trip, she said I already knew everything that she knew. I obviously didn't—certainly not as much as her mom, Linda.

Linda also found Jacob Samuel Ishach in the deportation records and the list of people murdered in the Shoah compiled by Yad Vashem, the Holocaust Museum in Israel. Most significantly Linda also discovered another Jacob Ishach. Jacob Isaac Ishach was listed in the Bulgarian Police registry compiled in 1942, but not in the deportation records from 1943. Emily sent me copies of the microfilmed registry entries for both Jacob Isaac and Jacob Samuel Ishach. It told their ages, the people in their households, their occupations, the color of their hair and eyes, and it supplied pictures. The entries are hard to read and blurry. There's also no picture of Jacob Samuel. I later learned that this probably meant relatives of his took the picture out of the register and kept it for themselves as a memorial in Israel. There is a shadowy picture of Jacob Isaac. Half of his face is blacked out, typical of what happens with microfilm. It's as if he's looking out of deep shadows. The existence of the picture in the register likely means there was nobody left to remember him.

What Kind of Past

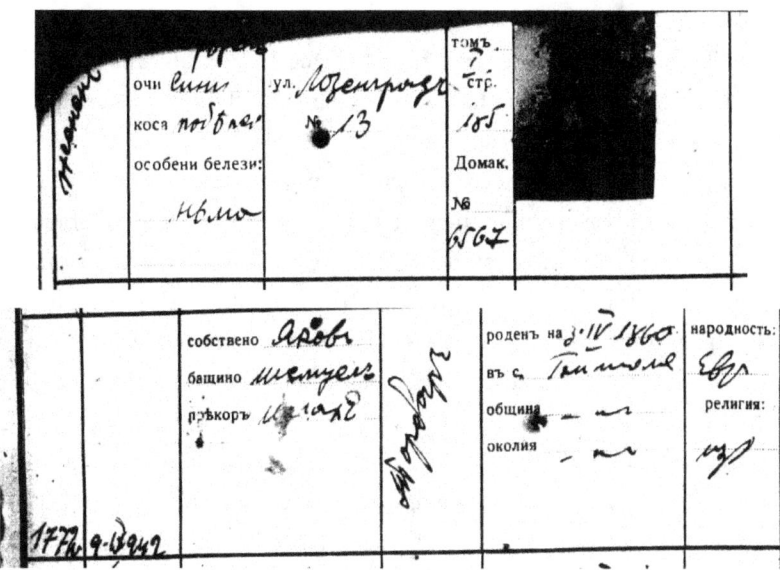

Jacob Samuel Ishach's entry in the microfilmed copy of the 1942 Bulgarian Police Registry. (Courtesy of Yad Vashem)

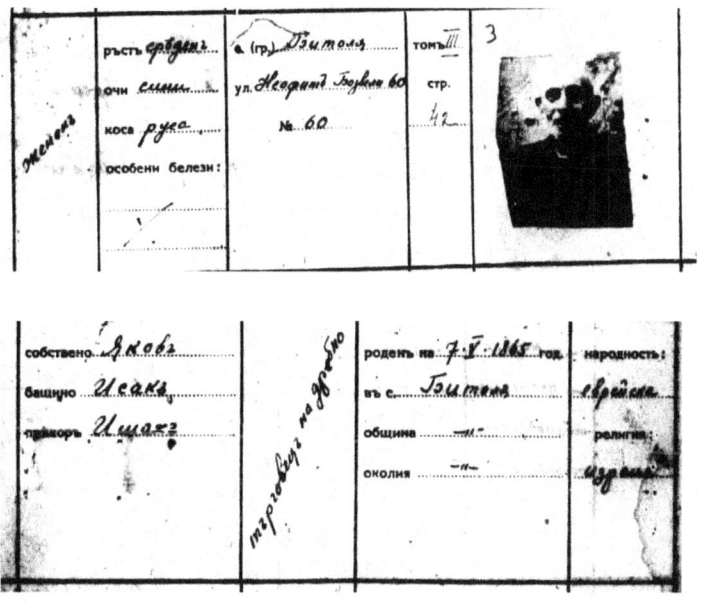

Jacob Isaac Ishach's entry in the microfilmed copy of the 1942 Bulgarian Police Registry. (Courtesy of Yad Vashem)

The Bulgarian Police Registry of Bitola is a remarkable document. It's chilling realizing the lengths to which the Bulgarians went in order to identify all the Jews of the town. Apparently, the pictures make the document unique in Holocaust archival materials.

By another coincidence, I'd seen the original document five years earlier while visiting Yad Vashem as part of a trip to Israel celebrating my in-laws' 50th wedding anniversary. The book was at eye-height on the end of a plastic display cabinet. I read the exhibit and realized it was from my grandfather's town. The coincidence struck me, but I couldn't read the Cyrillic text, and none of the pictures on the visible pages looked like family. Now, I really wish I had dug deeper then and learned more.

Jacob Samuel, who lived at 13 Lozengrad, was born in 1860. According to my father's memory, the age was correct. Jacob Samuel's wife, Sihul, was a year older than he. If they married after my grandfather's mother died around 1900, Sihul would have been a little old to start a second family. According to the police registry, Jacob Samuel worked as a "peddler." The Police Registry said Jacob Isaac was born in 1865, a little younger than my father remembers. He worked as a "merchant." His wife, Bochora, was fourteen years his junior. The younger wife makes a second family more likely.

While we were in our hotel in Thessaloniki, I read *The Jews of Monastir* by Schlomo Alboher, a book Maja, the curator of the Holocaust Museum gave me. In it I found a reference to Jacob Ishach applying for a permit to immigrate, or make Aliyah, to Palestine in 1929.

> On May 26, 1929, Leon Kamchi turned to Ovidia Hazan in Jerusalem and told him that he was taking care of obtaining Aliyah permits for Jews from Monastir. As part of the process, he was in touch with the English consul in Skopje and the Zionist Federation in Belgrade. He asked that Hazan try to obtain a permit for Jacob Ischak, 69 years old, his wife Behorah, 48, and their 2 daughters through the federation in Jerusalem. They had 500 pounds each. His brother in New York helped them. The daughters were seamstresses and could find work in a clothing factory in Israel.

This was Jacob Isaac Ishach. Being 69 years old in 1929, his birthday would have been 1860, different than the date listed in the Bulgarian Registry, but fitting my father's memory. After World War One, Palestine was under British control. Entry was limited. It was much easier to get a permit if you had 500 pounds per person. Five hundred Egyptian pounds in 1929 is worth about $44,000 in today's US dollars (2022). That means he had the equivalent of $160,000 in today's money with which to emigrate to Palestine. He was well off—something that was unusual for a Jew from this area during the inter-war years. Maybe Kamhi had gotten it slightly wrong, and it was Jacob's son (my grandfather Victor) in New York, rather than a brother? At least, we now knew that Jacob Isaac had two daughters!

Flying home, we transferred planes in Munich. I never thought I'd say it, but, "Thank God for the Germans." They provided free computers with Internet in the airport. Until then, I'd just worked through my phone. Going back to the 1943 German deportation lists, I noticed people who didn't have the same last name as the head of household could still be in the same listing. I found Jacob Isaac's wife, Bechora on line 1583. She lived in the house of Mois Kamchi and his wife Hana. It's reasonable to assume that Hana was her daughter. So, we possibly had the name of one of Jacob and Bechora's daughters. It's also reasonable to assume that Jacob was dead by this time. Otherwise, Bechora would have been living with him.

I grew up knowing some things about my great grandfather, but not enough to be able to pick between Jacob Isaac and Jacob Samuel. I was learning a lot, but what I learned created more questions. From Emily's emails, I gathered that her mom leaned towards Jacob Samuel being our ancestor. Looking at the information, I wasn't so sure. Isaac is my father's name.

What I Knew About Jacob

Names are important in my family. My grandfather's kids all named their eldest children Victor or Victoria to honor him. I've also always known that my great grandfather's name Jacob runs through the family via my father's older brother, my Uncle Jack, his children, and grandchildren.

My dad knew that his grandfather Jacob, "Poppa Grande," had been born around 1860. My great uncle Morris, who was both Jacob's nephew and his son-in-law, said Jacob was "an alderman" in Ottoman Monastir. He took care of the Jewish community. There are stories about how he supplied passports to help people emigrate—the best-known being Louis Russo, who ended up becoming the most financially successful Monastirli in New York. My dad figured out that Jacob was probably a *Mouktar* under the Ottomans. I found out that *Mouktars* served as local mayors. They took care of official documents and relations with the government for their village or neighborhood. So, the family stories made sense.

We don't know when Jacob married his first wife, Anna Negrin, my great grandmother. Nor do we know much about her. Born in 1889, my grandfather was Anna and Jacob's first child. They named him Victor and Haim ("life," in Hebrew) for being the first live birth after five stillbirths or miscarriages. If Jacob and Anna married at about 18 years old, math says that this would be possible, but it would have been awful. After Victor, they didn't have another child until my great aunt Vida, also named for "life," was born fourteen years later in 1902.

Other stories about Jacob tell us he sent his family in New York silver spoons, jewelry, knives, and blackberry jam. I have one of the silver spoons engraved with "VY" for his son. (My original objective of our 2018 trip was to bring my dad Macedonian blackberry jam and a locally made silver spoon). I also remember my father having a gold ring Jacob sent. My cousin Madeline talked about silver jewelry she played with as a kid. My Aunt Annie, my dad's oldest sister and Madeline's mom, used to write letters to her grandfather. This means that she was writing in Ladino, Judeo-Spanish, and probably using a script called Solitreo, which is only used for Ladino. My father remembers a story, probably from my great uncle Morris, of Jacob having a "house by the sea." It was likely in Salonica.

There were also some not-so-nice stories about Jacob. One tells about when Victor was a boy, Jacob slapped him so hard he left fingerprints on his cheek. Another story about Jacob, probably the one that most effected the family, was how he never told Victor that his mother Anna died a year after he left Monastir. Jacob also didn't tell Victor that he remarried and raised a second family. Victor found out in a coffee shop in New York City when he came to the US from Canada in 1910. He was understandably very angry. A rupture resulted between father and son. It was finally repaired, maybe by Aunt Vida, Victor's much younger sister, coming to New York ten years later, in 1920.

How the family heard about Jacob's death is another story. I have a mental picture transmitted through my father of Victor and my grandmother bent over the kitchen table reading a letter. It's the winter of 1943. They're living on Wilkens Avenue in the Bronx. Wrapped in many envelopes, the note took a year to make it from behind enemy lines, through war zones, to New York. Victor was skeptical of how it could have reached him, and whether the contents were true. The letter said that his father, Jacob, died "peacefully" of "natural causes." It arrived about eight months after the deportation and murder of all the Jews from Bitola. No one in New York yet knew their fate. That wouldn't happen until after the War's end.

Several questions surround this story. Who wrote the letter? Was it written before or after the deportation? Why would the writer say "peacefully, of natural causes," if written before? How did it come from Fascist occupied Macedonia to New York in the middle of the War? And, after my family received it, what happened to the letter?

If the letter was written before the deportation, any Jewish neighbor, or friend, could have composed it. After March of '43, one of the several Jewish doctors and pharmacists who avoided deportation could have penned it. If it were written after the deportation, a Christian, or Muslim friend was likely the author—but it's unlikely that person would be able to write in Ladino. Maybe the correspondent wrote in French, another language my grandfather and many people from Bitola spoke? The letter no longer exists. I've asked my father, his sister, my Aunt Beck, and my cousins. In the younger generations, nobody remembers seeing it, but that scene is painted in all our heads. My cousin Madeline described it almost exactly the same way as my dad. Madeline must have gotten the story from her mom. As for how the mysterious document made its way out, later research gave me some theories, but no solid answers.

My family talked about the letter often, but rarely mentioned Jacob's second family. If their fate was brought up, I can picture in my mind my Aunt Annie raising her hand and shaking her head as if to avoid the sight of those thoughts. Part of that avoidance was likely denial. The older generations didn't want to definitively know that those family members were killed in the Holocaust. Not knowing left some small window of hope. I think that Jacob's negative image within the family helped make that type of attitude easier. The guilt of his bad actions was transferred to the "second family."

In talking to my dad and Aunt Beck, I found out that Victor never talked about his past, at least not to them, his two youngest children. The stories about Victor's father and his youth came through my grandmother.

The immediate family tree I knew growing up.

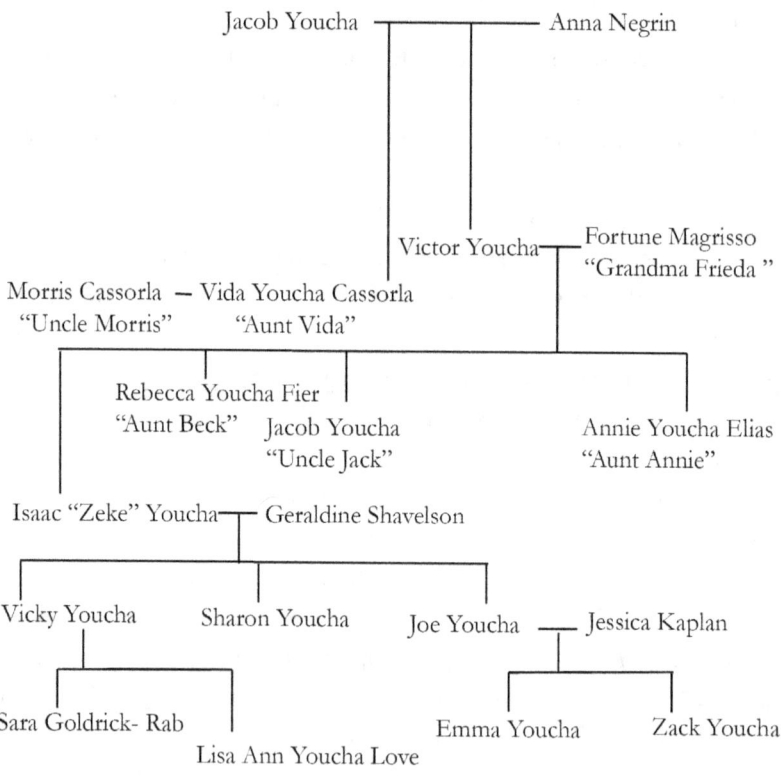

These stories were in my head as I tried to fit them into what I was learning about Jacob Samuel and Jacob Isaac Ishach.

The more I thought about it, the more I felt that Jacob Isaac Ishach was my ancestor—not Jacob Samuel. The family stories just lined up so much better with what we knew about Jacob Isaac. His "merchant" listing in the Bulgarian Registry correlated to the family story of his relative affluence and ability to send fancy gifts to his son and grandchildren during the Great Depression. Jacob Isaac's not being on the deportation list but listed on the earlier Police Registry matched the family's story about Victor receiving the letter in the winter of 1943 saying that his father, Jacob, died peacefully, of natural causes. I just needed to find something that would connect Jacob Isaac to our family.

New York Arlington, Virginia 2019

Finding Sharon's Family Tree

I grew up in an old Dutch farmhouse about an hour north of New York City. My mom grew up two towns over and became a journalist. My dad grew up a street kid in Brooklyn and the Bronx. After serving in the Navy during World War Two, he went to school on the G.I. Bill and became a probation officer, social worker, professor of medicine, and a therapist. One of my sisters, Sharon, became a physician; my eldest sister, Vicky, a developmental specialist for very young children. I'm the youngest. I remember the house always being the center of extended family gatherings. At various times after Passover or Thanksgiving, my dad recorded the family conversations, first on reel-to-reel tapes, later on cassettes. I remember being just tall enough to peek over the edge of the dining room table and watch my aunts, uncles, grandmother, great aunt, and great uncle go back and forth. The conversation would switch between English and Ladino—Judeo Spanish. I guess I was about 5 years old; it was the first time I realized that parts of my family could speak a different language.

My dad still lives in that house. After we got back from our 2018 Balkan trip, I went looking for the family recordings. All the tapes and stereo equipment were kept in the base of one bookcase. I tore it apart and found nothing. Frustrated, but still with a lot of energy, I decided to go through a nearby cabinet.

After sorting through a 78 record album of *On the Town*, as well as the front pages of the *New York Times* announcing Kennedy's assassination and Armstrong landing on the moon, I reached way in back and felt a rolled-up piece of heavy paper. Pulling it out, I realized what it was. When we were kids, my sister Sharon (the one that would become a doctor) made a family tree. I was about six at the time, six years younger than Sharon, and jealous that, like our mom the journalist, she got to interview people. Later in life, Sharon needed to create another family tree and forgot this earlier version existed. I remembered. We looked for it several times over the years, but never found it. Now, it appeared.

Unrolling the paper, I saw that Sharon compiled it as a project in eighth grade. Sure enough, Victor's father was listed as Jacob Isaac Youcha. In a Sephardic male name, traditionally the middle name is the first name of the father, the same for an unmarried woman. For a married woman, her middle name is her husband's first name. Sharon must have gotten the information on the tree from our grandmother, Great Aunt Vida, Great Uncle Morris, or from Aunt Annie, our dad's oldest sister. Since names are important in my family, having a "Jacob Isaac" as an ancestor made sense. When my grandparents named my father Isaac and my Uncle Jack, Jacob, they were keeping those names alive in the family. We don't have any Samuels in our immediate family. The tree also told us that Jacob's grandmothers shared the same last name. The source of the information remembered the relationship, but not the specific name. Sharon listed it as a question mark. Finding the tree, I felt that Sharon left the family a real gift. It was an especially eerie feeling because Shar passed away three years before I rediscovered her work.

Youcha Family Photo. (Youcha family photo around 2010)

What Kind of Past 23

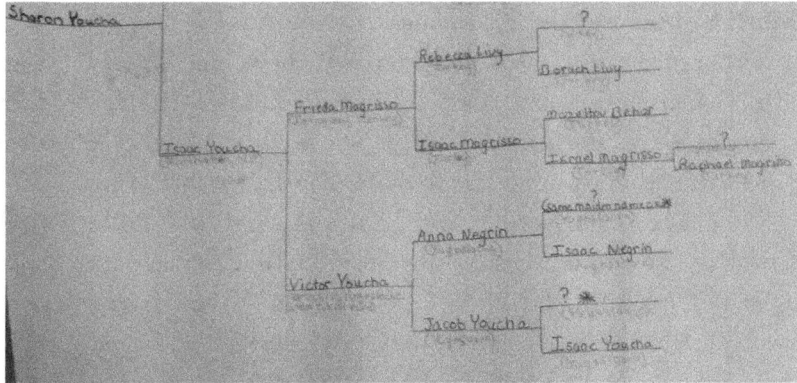

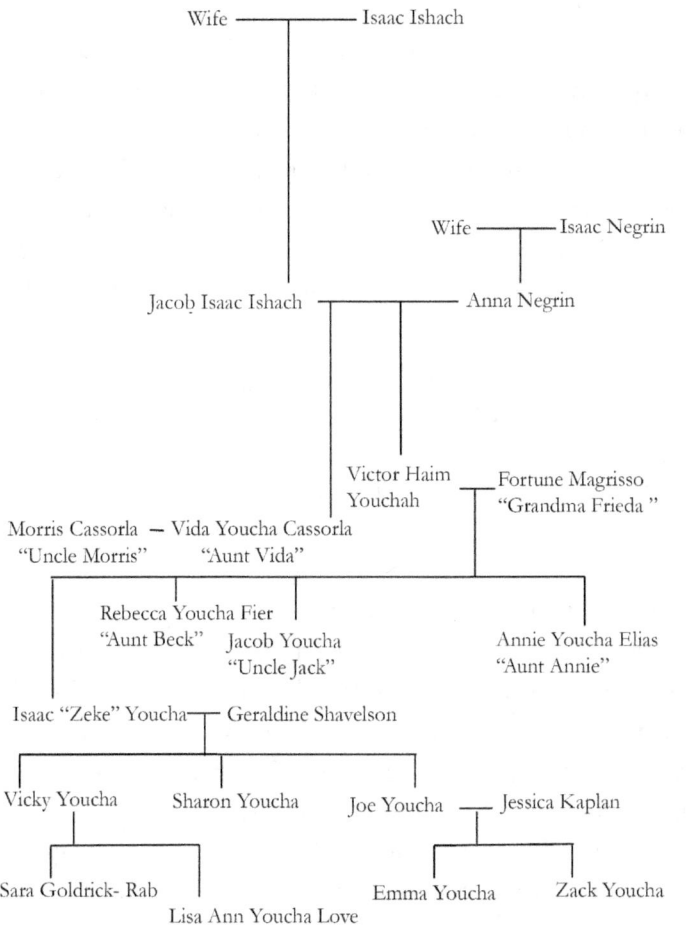

Above: My sister Sharon's family tree from 1968. (Joe Youcha photo) Below: The family tree after discovering Sharon's tree.

Mark Cohen and the Holocaust Museum

About the same time, I found Sharon's family tree, I read through Mark Cohen's book, *Last Century of a Sephardic Community*. It's a thorough, complete history of Jewish Monastir. The notes and bibliography also provide tremendous, invaluable resources for a researcher. On page 100 of Cohen's book, he quotes from the *Bulletin Semestrial de l'Alliance Israelite Universelle 1900*, an organization that played a large role in my grandfather's life, "Jacob Ishach Victim of a Blood Libel." "A traveling merchant, Jacob Ishach, was beaten and looted by peasants." A blood libel, saying that Jews used Christian blood to make Matzoh, is a lie used for ages to provoke Christian attacks against Jews. Could this be our Jacob? There were no family stories about such a thing happening, but that didn't rule out the possibility.

The National Library of Israel has copies of the Alliance Bulletins online. Written in French, the 1900 Bulletin describes Jacob as a "negotiant ambulant." Looking up this phrase in a period dictionary, I found that rather than meaning a traveling merchant or salesman, as it does today, a more correct translation for this document would be "peddler." In the 1941 German and Bulgarian documents, Jacob Samuel's occupation is listed as a peddler. He was most likely the victim of this 1900 beating.

> Cependant la calomnie exerce ses ravages. Un négociant ambulant, Jacob Ischah, se rendit comme d'habitude dans un village éloigné de 1 heure 1/2 de Monastir. Il fut battu et pillé par les paysans. Le colporteur Haym Lévi fut battu et

Entry in the Alliance Israelite Universelle 1900 Bulliten.
(Retrieved from National Library of Israel)

Picture of Jacob Isaac Ishach

After my cousin, Emily, sent me the shadowy picture of Jacob Isaac from a microfilmed copy of the 1942 Bulgarian Police Registry, I wanted a better version. Soon after we got back from our 2018 trip, I visited the library at the US Holocaust Memorial Museums (USHMM) in Washington, DC, about twenty minutes from my house in Arlington, Virginia.

Without an appointment, I walked into the photograph archives. Through the generosity of the archivist who stopped what she was doing to help me, I looked through all the pictures of the Jews from Bitola, which the Museum has put online. I spent hours looking at them. Many of these faces are the same ones displayed as you walk into the Holocaust Museum in Skopje. They are the faces of many people my great grandfather must have known well.

Over several years, USHMM researchers collected related materials from different archives in Macedonia and Israel. These pictures were part of it. A man named Isaac Nehama, a Greek Holocaust survivor whose family came from Bitola, volunteered at the USHMM for years matching names to the pictures. Everyone I spoke to about him loved him. Sadly, he passed away a couple of years before I showed up at the USHMM Archives. Mr. Nehama lived in Bethesda, Maryland, ten miles from my house, the town where my wife grew up. I just missed him.

Jacob Isaac's photo wasn't in the online collection. However, in the USHMM photograph archive they did have scans of the Bulgarian Police Registry in the Yad Vashem collection. I got a copy of Jacob Isaac's entry. A low-resolution scan, it's better than the microfilm version and shows Jacob as a real person, out of the shadows. Even without Sharon's family tree, I'd know this man was a Youcha. He has the family cheeks. Still, I wanted to find a better version of the photo. I couldn't take the original from the book now in Yad Vashem, as other people did to remember their relatives, but I wanted as good a version as I could get.

Through the USHMM photo archivist, I contacted Yad Vashem and got their highest quality scan of Jacob Isaac's Bulgarian police registry entry and picture. Joseph Benatov translated all the particulars. To my astonishment, I learned that Jacob had blond hair and blue eyes. Not what I'd grown up thinking of as typical Youcha coloring. I couldn't tell from the photo. It wasn't clear enough for that. Our eldest, Emma, has blue eyes. I knew they came from my mother's side of the family. Maybe they came from both?

The blue eyes in our family break a coloring stereotype for Sephardic Jews. Emma pointed me to an article about Jew's "White supremacy problem" by Devin Naar, a professor of Sephardic Studies at the University of Washington. I'd always felt the difference between Sephardic and Ashkenazi Jews but thought it was just because there were so many more Eastern European Jews than Sephardim. In his article, Naar writes about the racial stereotyping, and racism, practiced by Jews against Jews. He tells the story of how in 1909 Jews from the Ottoman Empire (Syria) were classified by a US judge as "Asiatic," and therefore ineligible for US citizenship at the time. That ruling was later retracted, and all Jews were classified as "Hebrew," which let us be White—when it came to US citizenship. It was a lot think about.

These photos raise so many questions. The picture of Jacob Isaac was likely taken only a few months before he died. It looks like a studio picture. For sure, he is seated. He's thin, wearing glasses, and what looks like a traditional shirt. There might also be a bandage on his neck. Does this give us a hint of what disease killed him? Was he a smoker, like others in the family? Was throat cancer catching up with him when he was almost 80? We'll never know, but I wonder. The picture captures Jacob at the end of his life and in the middle of an unimaginably horrific time. I wanted to see if I could find out about his earlier life. There had to be more information.

Close up of Jacob Isaac from a better resolution scan. (Courtesy of United States Holocaust Memorial Museum)

Jacob Isaac Ishach's entry in the Bulgarian Police Registry. (Courtesy of Yad Vashem)

Rante Takes Up the Cause

Bojan Rantasa's business card reads, "mastermind and guide." It does not lie. Bojan, who usually goes by "Rante," guided us through Macedonia during our 2018 Balkan trip. Usually, Rante's work involves bicycle touring; we were lucky enough to get him on one of his "regular" tour jobs. Soon after we returned from our trip, my dad came down to visit. I sent Rante a picture of my dad eating the Macedonian blackberry jam Rante found us. My dad was using a silver spoon we found in Skopje. (I don't think it really mattered that the spoon was probably originally for a christening...) It turned out it was Rante's birthday (June 30th). He said it was the best present he received that year. It was nothing compared to the gifts he had already given me and my family and those he would continue to give us.

I sent Rante a copy of the emails I earlier sent to my family. He then provided the link to the Facebook pages with the book the archivist used to find Lozengrad Street. That information and Jacob Isaac's police registry, along with my wife Jessica's knowledge of Cyrillic, got us to the street being listed on "Line 54" of the document, but we could get no further. Rante soon replied with the address where Jacob Isaac lived in 1942 and a current photograph of the house from Google. It turns out we walked right by it when we were looking for 13 Lozengrad Street. The address is currently called Dimitrie Tucovikj 60. It runs parallel to the street where the archivist and his family live.

Wanting to continue the research, I asked Rante for the contact information of the woman leading the cemetery preservation, as well as that of the archivist we met. He gave them to me but said that since he was already doing the research, he'd like to continue. I offered to pay him. He refused and said that maybe, at some point, I could contribute to his "bicycle parts fund." He also gave me a list of questions to answer. He was going to "make a nice bike ride" to Bitola and would "stop in" at the archives. Soon he shared with me a Google spreadsheet with an outline of my family history. I filled in the details I knew, and Rante was off.

Within a couple of days, he visited the Holocaust Museum and Municipal Archives in Skopje where he found a complete list of all the documents pertaining to the Jews of Bitola which were in the possession of any Macedonian municipal agency. Many were in the Bitolan Archives. In the spreadsheet, Rante outlined what he discovered about each person who could possibly have been in my family. Traveling to the Bitolan Archives would have to wait a couple of weeks because of his guiding work.

Meeting Goran

During this time, I emailed our trip leader Joseph asking for help. One of the first things Joseph did was connect me to Goran Sadikario, the head of the Holocaust Fund in Macedonia. Goran's grandparents were originally from Bitola and were among the approximately sixty Jews from the town to survive World War Two.

When I got in touch with Goran, he promised to have his staff look through their records to see if they could find anything pertaining to my family. He also mentioned that he might be coming to Washington, DC, for a conference at the Holocaust Museum in the Spring of 2019. He did make the trip, and over a very nice brunch, we speculated that we were likely cousins. This is something that happens a lot when Jews originally from Monastir meet. We also talked about the educational projects he planned for the Museum in Skopje and whether Jessica and I could help in any way.

Our brunch conversation touched on the different sources of information that were left in the country, including the scanned and translated tombstones from the Jewish Cemetery in Bitola. Goran's grim smile told me that because of political, religious, and interpersonal background, getting the desired information wasn't going to be simple. I'm used to designing and building educational and social programs in the States. It's not usually a straightforward process, but I was to learn how much more complicated and layered things could be in the small nation of North Macedonia.

Jacob Aroesti's Book

While researching, I found a *Yizkor* book online by Jacob Aroesti for the Jewish community of Bitola. *Yizkor*, or works of memory, make sure those murdered in the Holocaust will not be forgotten. Aroesti was a Bitolan Jew who survived the War—one of very few who returned to Bitola. Written in 1959, with the help of two Christian brothers who were historians, the book gives a history of the town. Using Serbian records of the Jewish community, as well as the Bulgarian Police Records and Deportation lists, the work gives all the known facts about each Jew of the community. Mark Cohen rediscovered the book in 2000 at the end of his research for *The Last Century*. Writing an introduction for the online version of Aroesti's book, Cohen calls it "the most obscure Holocaust memorial book ever produced." Only two typewritten copies were made. Written in Serbo-Croat with Latin letters, Cohen calls the book "purposefully obscure." It is written in Serbo-Croat with Latin letters. Who would read it? Not the Monastirlis in Israel who spoke Hebrew. Not the Monastirlis in America who spoke English. Not the Monastirlis in Chile who spoke Spanish. Aroesti could have written it in Ladino, which was spoken by some people in all those countries, but he didn't. Cohen thinks by writing in Serbo-Croatian, Aroesti despaired of finding an audience. And that the book "expects no readers." It's "a mute sign, a tombstone for thousands."

Digging into the book and again using Jessica's knowledge of the Cyrillic alphabet and Google Translate, I found Jacob Isaac's wife Bechora in the household of Anna and Mois Kamhi. Despite a thorough search, I didn't find Jacob Isaac. I pointed Rante towards the book. He thought it was likely the "big book" he heard about being in the Bitolan Archives. He would be there soon.

Not only was Aroesti's book in the Bitolan Archives, but the archives' collection also contained the notes he used to prepare the book. On that first visit, Rante reconnected with Dimitar, the archivist we met on the street, but he only got a quick look at the materials. However, in Aroesti's notes, Rante found Jacob Isaac, Bechora and their daughters, Anna and Roza. Jacob was listed as a seller of "fine things." Roza had married and gone to Greece, and Anna had married and stayed in Bitola. Everything lined up with the family stories and the information on the German/Bulgarian deportation lists. We also now knew the second daughter's name, Roza, and a little bit about her.

241.   Битола,   2.750.1.241./855-857

ИШАХ ШАЛОМ ИСАК, ул.М.Крстиќ бр.24, роден 1906г.во Битола од
мајка Рахел и татко Шалом, по занимање бил шивач; сопругата
Ишах И.АЛЕГРА родена 1914г.во Скопје била шивачка; синот Ишах
И.ШАЛОМ роден 1938г; синот Ишах И.БЕНЈАМИН роден 1939г; мајката
Ишах Ш.РАХЕЛ родена 1884г.во Битола била шивачка.Одведени во
логор.   листови 3
Податоци во книге 1, 4 и 6.

242.   Битола,   2.750.1.242./858-862

ИШАХ САМУЕЛ ЈАКОВ, ул.Сремска бр.13, роден 04.01.1861г.во Битола по занимање бил старинар; сопругата Ишах Ј.СУНКУ родена 04.
03.1859г.во Битола била домаќинка; синот Ишах Ј.ЈОСЕФ роден
1897г.бил чевлар, бил воен заробеник, се иселил во Израел; сопругата Ишах Јо.РАШЕЛ (   ) родена 20.11.1898г.во Битола
од мајка Касорла Мирјам и татко Касорла Елијау била домаќинка;
синот Ишах Јо.ЈАКОВ роден 04.07.1921г.бил чевлар; ќерките Ишах
Јо.РЕБЕКА родена 14.03.1927г.и Ишах Јо.МИРЈАМ родена 05.01.
1930г.биле шивачки помошнички; ќерките Ишах Јо.СОЛ родена 08.
08.1932г.и Ишах Јо.ДОНА родена 12.06.1935г; Ишах Јо.ЕЛИЈАУ роден 1931г.-починал 1931г; Ишах Јо.МАЗАЛТО родена 1937г; Ишах Ј.
АЛЕГРА родена 1924г.била слугинка.Одведени во логор.
                                                   листови 5
Податоци во книге 1, 3 и 6.

243.   Битола,   2.750.1.243./863

ИШАХ И. ЈАКОВ, ул.Карађорђева бр.54, роден 1865г.бил трговец со
галантерија-починат; Ишах Ј.БОХОРА родена 1879г.била домаќинка;
Ишах Ј.АНА родена 1914г.била домаќинка-одведени во логор; Ишах
Ј.РОЗА родена 1912г.била домаќинка-се иселила во Грција.
                                                   лист 1
Податоци во книге 3.

244.   Битола,   2.750.1.244./864-865

ИШАХ К. ЈАКОВ, ул.Синагогина бр.14, роден 1906г.по занимање бил
торбар; Ишах Ј.КЛАРА родена 1905г.била домаќинка; Ишах Ј.ЈОСЕФ
роден 1930г; Ишах Ј.ДОЈА родена 1935г.Одведени во логор.
                                                   листови 2

245.   Битола,   2.750.1.245./866-868

ИШАХ ИСАК ЈОСЕФ, ул.Војвода Путник бр.3, роден 1910г.во Битола
по занимање бил шивачки работник; сопругата Ишах Ј.ВИДА родена
1915г.во Битола била домаќинка; ќерките Ишах Ј.ЕСТЕР родена
1935г.и Ишах Ј.МАЗАЛТО родена 1936г.биле ученички; ќерките
Ишах Ј.ЕЛВИРА родена 1938г.и Ишах Ј.РАХЕЛ родена 1942г.во
Битола.Одведени во логор.   листови 3
Податоци во книге 1, 5 и 6.

Jacob Aroesti's typewritten notes listing Jacob Isaac and the family in entry 243. (Courtesy of Macedonian National Archives, Bitola)

What Kind of Past 31

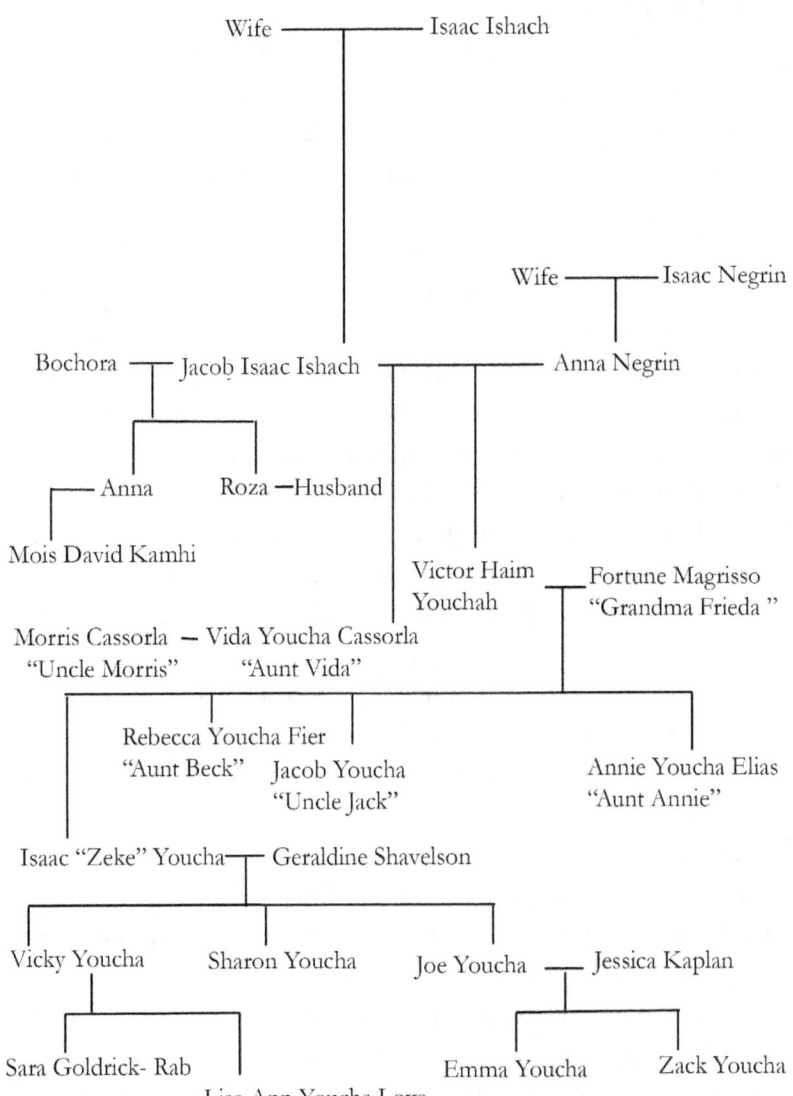

The family tree with Jacob's second family.

The Manaki Brothers

When I visited the USHMM library searching for a better photograph of Jacob Isaac, I found it, along with hundreds of others. I wondered, "How did these pictures exist?" Why was the Bulgarian Police Registry regarded as unique in Holocaust studies because it contained photographs of the victims?

I learned that the Aromanian brothers Yanaki and Milton Manaki took thousands of photographs of Monastir, as well as early movies. Aromanians are yet another ethnic minority of the Balkans. Supposedly descended from the Roman soldiers who defended the empire, they lived in their own communities and spoke their own language. The Manakis were born in one of those villages, Avdella, near the town of Greneva. Then part of the Ottoman Empire, now it's part of Greece.

By 1890, Yanaki, the older brother, attended an Aromanian boarding school in Monastir, about 150 km from Greneva. The brothers started a photographic studio in Monastir by 1905. They soon made the first moving pictures in the Ottoman Empire and were the official photographers of whomever ruled Monastir/Bitola. The Manakis' pictures connect the story of my family. Through their images, we see Monastir as it moved from being under Ottoman, Serbian, Yugoslav, and Bulgarian rule. We also get to see the people.

Between them, Milton and Yanaki documented every major event in the history of Monastir/Bitola from 1905 through World War Two. After World War One, their studio destroyed, they opened a movie theatre, where in the 1930s, Zionist films were likely shown.

By 1935, only Milton was left in Bitola. Yanaki left Bitola that year for Thessaloniki. From my standpoint, Milton performed one more important job. In the latter half of 1942, the Bulgarian occupiers commissioned Milton to photograph all the Jews who couldn't supply photographs of their own for the Police Registry. This is why we have the photograph of my great grandfather, Jacob, and so many people from his community.

Almost 20,000 of the Manaki's photographs and documents survive in the Bitolan Archives. Milton only labeled 6,000 late in his life. A book recently privately printed in Macedonia documents the pictures that Milton indicated were "Jewish." At some point after the war, someone put the Manaki photographs of Bitola's Jews into an album. Milton died in 1964. Jacob Aroesti did his research in the mid to late 1950s. They likely created the photo album together. The handwriting in the album certainly looks like Aroesti's.

In his time at the Bitolan archive, Rante discovered the Manaki Brothers, Yanaki and Milton. At least for me he did. When Rante examined the Manaki/Aroesti photo album, he noticed that at the bottom of each photograph is a number in pencil. He figured out its meaning. The numbers on the photographs correspond to the numbers identifying the families in Jacob Aroesti's Yizkor book. Rante told Goran, the Director at the Holocaust Museum in Skopje, about the relationship and blew him away. Holocaust researchers always wondered what the numbers on the photos meant. We now can put faces to the names. Isaac Nehama, volunteering at the US Holocaust Memorial Museum, did much of this work from his memory, but now we had a more direct source.

I learned that I was watching Rante do something he does very well, making connections—connections between facts and connections between people. We were finding information about Jacob and his second family. We were getting photographs and bits of information. A better

Milton and Yanaki Manaki, Self-Portrait. (Courtesy of Macedonian National Archives, Bitola)

picture was developing, but I wanted to know more about Jacob and more about his first family, my family. I especially wanted to find out more about my grandfather, Victor. His not talking about his past left his years before coming to America as a bare outline. I wanted to fill it in. All I knew about Victor came from family stories and the immigration documents my cousin Linda discovered. I wondered if there was more.

More Family Stories About My Grandfather, Victor

Around the time of my Bar Mitzvah in 1975, I remember my father telling his mother that I was a lot like Victor, his father. Although not particularly religious, I would smile if I saw in a window a pair of candles lit for the Sabbath on a Friday night. It's still a fair description. Even though he died 17 years before I was born, when my dad was only 17, Victor has always been a warm and influential presence in my life.

Beloved in the family as I said earlier, each of his surviving children named their first born either Victor or Victoria. At family gatherings when I was very little, I got a kick out of yelling, "Hey Vic!" and watching four people turn around. (I was probably put up to it by my cousin Robbie…)

Aunt Beck, Victor's youngest daughter, remembered as a little girl waiting for him on the street and running into his arms whenever she saw him. He was polite, teaching my dad "how to act," how to treat people. I learned from my father, as he learned from his, to stay on the outside when walking with a lady on the sidewalk.

Named after my mother's father, I was always told that my middle name, Michael, was to honor my dad's Uncle Morris. Morris was my Aunt Vida's husband—Victor's brother-in-law and first cousin. My father didn't know his grandfathers and I didn't know mine. I've always wished I could have met them. I think my dad feels the same about his.

The family knew the basic timeline of Victor's life. He was born in Monastir when Macedonia was still Ottoman. At some point he contracted smallpox. He witnessed a murder around the time of his Bar Mitzvah. This forced him to leave Monastir for an Agricultural school in Tunisia run by the *Alliance Israelite Universelle*—the school system designed by mostly French Jews to educate the "downtrodden" Sephardic Jews.

From Tunisia, my grandmother said that her husband went to Palestine to be a "pioneer" farmer. As a young man, I romanticized about Victor working on an early Kibbutz. It's a nice idea, but Uncle Morris said Victor never went to Palestine. Regardless, Victor ended up in Canada where he supposedly worked on the Canadian Railroad. He also dramatically entered the United States from Canada. He could have been arrested on kidnapping charges but wasn't. Once in New York, he soon learned about his mother's death and his father's remarriage.

In 1915, Victor married my grandmother, Fortune Magrisso, a 21-year-old woman originally from Kir Kilisse (now Kirklareli, Turkey) on the plain of Thrace between Bulgaria and Constantinople (now Istanbul). She came to New York fleeing the Balkan Wars. Grandma's first name was Fortune in Ladino, Mazel Tov in Hebrew, Frieda in English. Many names, but I always knew her as the same tough, loving woman. A year after their marriage, the children started arriving with Annie, named after Victor's mother, Anna. (There's even a story that Grandma was pregnant before she married, and that she broke with Victor when she found out she was going to have his child. Victor then begged her to marry him. The personalities of my grandmother and grandfather would certainly make the story feasible, but the math on their marriage date and my Aunt Annie's birth proves it wrong.)

Tragically, Victor and Fortune lost two sons, always called by the family "the first" Jacob and Isaac. The first Jacob died when he was about three. The first Isaac was eight when he was hit by a car and died in my grandmother's arms waiting in a hospital that was too busy to see him. Victor came home from work that day to find out his son was dead. Four children, Annie, Jacob, Rebecca, and Isaac, my father, survived.

Victor was obviously well educated. He spoke about eight languages. And, his French was very good—a real "schoolboy" French. He was also good at math. A great family story tells how each child got an egg for breakfast. There wasn't one for Poppa, but it was OK. He'd just take $1/3$ from each of the four kids. The man understood fractions.

Not a tall man, at 5'2" my dad remembers him "towering" over 4'10" Fortune. In pictures, he's stocky, tending to round as he got older. Being sedentary worked for him. When my grandmother would ask to go somewhere, Victor would say he didn't want to travel. He was happy where he was, with the family. He didn't need to go anywhere. He had been enough places. He also liked to smoke. At the end of life, when his doctor told him to quit; he refused, saying it was his last pleasure. From Jacob's picture and the bandage on his throat, we can guess that smoking may have been what killed his father.

Victor enjoyed fishing. My dad tells stories of his father going out on "Party Boats" from Sheepshead Bay in Brooklyn and catching sacks of fish. They would clean them on the kitchen table and give fish to the family and neighbors. One of the few things I have of Victor's is his fishing reel.

One time my grandmother, Fortune, begged her husband to take her along fishing. Even though she lived most of her life in Brooklyn, being able to look at the ocean, she always got seasick or carsick. After her ocean crossing to get to America, she never wanted to go on water again.

This one time, Victor gave in and took his wife along. Before they cleared the breakwater, she was sick and lying in the cockpit of the boat. They couldn't turn around. She suffered all through the trip, blaming her husband for taking her. Even though she begged to go, he should know how sick it was going to make her! Knowing my grandmother, I think this story might describe a good part of their marriage.

As with all father/son relationships, my dad's interaction with his father had complications. My dad says that he always felt his father was distanced from him—likely because of the earlier death of his first two sons. Apparently, they never talked in-depth about anything serious. My grandmother said Victor was waiting until my dad and his brother, Uncle Jack, were grown. The opportunity for that conversation never came. This distancing between generations certainly effected my life.

With all these family stories, it's important to remember that Victor never spoke about his early life to my dad. Everything my dad learned was through his mother and maybe Annie, his oldest sister. Growing up, my father had what he calls, "big ears." What he overheard as a young, smart, curious child provides the source for many of my family's stories. At times while investigating these stories, the eyes of my eight-year-old father provided the lens. What did he hear? How did he interpret it?

Fortune, Annie, and Victor in 1920. (Youcha family photo)

And, how, as an adult, did he fit it into a narrative that made sense? The process of verifying and building out these family stories took me in very interesting directions.

Family Tree with "first" Jacob and Isaac.

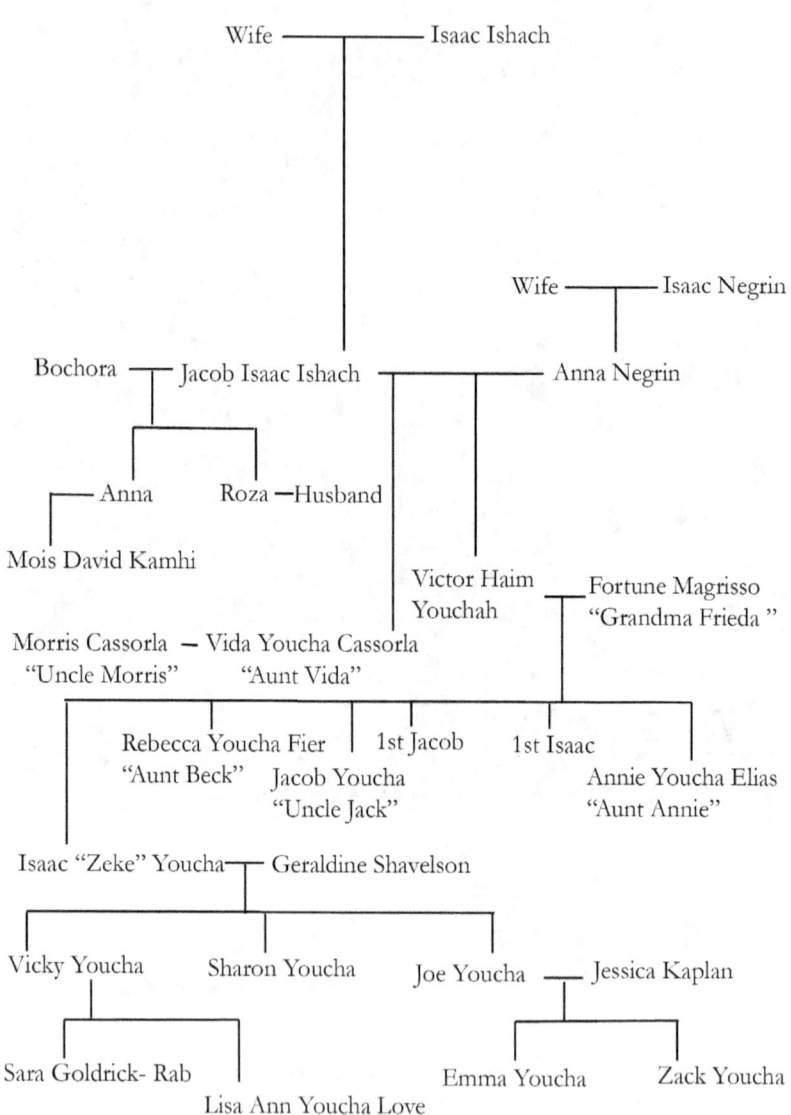

Music, Building Musical Instruments, and the Oud

Music and musical instruments have a major place in this story even though I'm not a musical person. As a kid, I wasted seven years of my piano teacher's time. A very talented musician, Arthur Krilov played oboe in a New York symphony; I'm afraid we talked more about baseball than piano. On top of that, just shy of 18 years old, I had an accident with a joiner, an unforgiving stationary woodworking machine. On my left hand, I ended up with part of a toe for the end of the index finger, as well as three other reduced and scarred digits. I just didn't think I could make music.

When my kids were growing up, they worked in the boat shop with me. Good sports, they weren't really interested in building wooden boats. Music interested them much more. So, we started building musical instruments. First, cigar box guitars and ukuleles, then repairing banjos and guitars. I found out friends were, or had been, luthiers. Very generous with tools, materials, and experience, I think they loved the idea that building instruments at least somewhat interested my kids.

It helped that my friend and mentor with whom I started the community-based wooden boat building programs at the Alexandria Seaport Foundation built musical instruments twenty years before I met him. Anything that could be constructed interested Bill Hunley. As Chief Naval Architect of the US Navy, he led the design and building of the most powerful ships in the world. He made guitars, violins, and banjos for his daughters when they wanted to learn music. He built homes when he needed a place to live. And he helped his community build lots and lots of small boats to help young people. Bill passed some partially completed instrument projects, tools, as well as a lot of raw materials to me and my kids.

Another one of my musical instrument friends is David Rapkievian, a well-respected maker of concert violins and violas. I met David through his wife, Carolyn, a traditional Armenian dancer, who happened to run the educational programming for the Smithsonian's National Museum of the American Indian. When the Museum opened, their first hands-on exhibits were boats and boat builders. Hawaiian, Inuit, and Ojibwa builders all came to DC. I ran the only wooden boat shop in town, so Carolyn and I connected and worked together over many years. Along the way we became good friends. At some point Carolyn and her husband, David, came over to our house for dinner. Since David's a luthier, Zack, then probably less than ten, proudly showed him a cigar box guitar we built recently. David promptly invited us to come visit his shop.

We did. Many, many times we drove from Virginia to Maryland and knocked on David's basement shop door. Currently fascinated with playing the oud, earlier in his life, David played and made premier balalaikas. Every visit, we'd get a concert on the oud, balalaika, or both. I remember him playing the balalaika while passing it around his waist. Sometimes, he'd open the shop door with a big smile on his face, oud in hand.

The oud began surfacing elsewhere in my life around this time. We saw one while visiting the Guitar Heroes exhibit at the Metropolitan Museum of Art in 2011. That was really what got Zack into the shop, wanting to build instruments. Then, as I got more interested in the music of my Sephardic heritage, I started listening to the music of Flory Jagoda who was originally from Sarajevo in Bosnia but only lived a few miles from my house in Northern Virginia. She played oud, along with the guitar. We even went to see Flory's apprentice, Susan Gaeta, perform with her group *Trio Sephardi* in March 2018—just before we went to the Balkans.

The oud gets described as a fretless lute. It's got a big bowl body made up of many thin strips of wood and a relatively short neck with a smooth fingerboard. Creating the correct tone doesn't depend on the instrument builder accurately placing a piece of fret wire, as in a guitar. Good tone depends upon the ear of the player and their fingers' memory of the notes' spacing on the fretboard. The ancestor of the lute, guitar, and mandolin and going back at least to the 8th century, some say back to prehistory with its first mention in Genesis, the oud travelled from Persia through the Middle East, Balkans, and all the way to Spain. The many branches of oud music include Armenian, Persian, and Azeri, but Turkish and Arabic styles currently dominate. Jews feel the oud's presence throughout Sephardic/Ladino music and even through traditional liturgical pieces.

All types of instruments fascinate my son Zack. David Rapkivian picked up on this and gave us an unfinished oud. It needed a lot of work, including a top and a fretboard. I admit the idea of fixing it didn't thrill me. We already had lots of projects on the bench. As Zack got busier during high school, we spent less time working together in the shop. The oud sat, waiting patiently. Around this time, 2016, I went through a series of deep tissue muscle massages that broke free all the scar tissue from the base of my skull, down my left arm and into my hand. Forty years after my injury on that joiner, I could really start using my left hand—even to play music on stringed instruments.

One Saturday at a local flea market, the neck of an instrument stuck out from underneath a table. For ten bucks, I bought a poorly made Arabic oud sized for a child. Its pegbox had been knocked off and the neck didn't line up correctly with the body. I talked to David about how to fix it. He relayed a technique for resetting oud necks used by Chris Pantzelos, an excellent luthier in Lowell, Massachusetts. This brutal method of cutting, wedging, and listening for the wood to crack, worked. I ended up with a playable oud and started plunking away. Even though Zack was now away at college, playing this instrument inspired me to put a new top on the oud body David gave us several years earlier. I was very glad that I'm a boat builder because working on an oud is like working on a boat. It's all curves, only smaller, with much finer tolerances. I probably used too many down and dirty boat building techniques in this repair, but I made the oud playable and started practicing more.

David pointed me to a book by his teacher, a well-known Lebanese oud player named Charbel Rouhana. It turned out that Charbel's book is not readily available in this country; quite the contrary. However, I found out by emailing the publisher in Lebanon that I could get a copy by contacting "Father Georges" at the Maronite Church in Washington, DC. Father Georges was a character. It was a parking lot purchase. Cash only. It turns out that Charbel's brother is a Maronite bishop, and all the family friends in the church provide a distribution network for Charbel's music books. Overly excited with the book in hand, I got a speeding ticket on the way home—no small achievement when driving a 1983 Mercedes Benz diesel station wagon! David gave me some pointers, and I really started practicing. David also said I should have a better oud. For a reasonable price, he sold me a Moroccan style instrument whose bridge had pulled off, taking some of its soundboard with it. I got in touch with Chris, the luthier in Lowell, and he talked me through the repair. Just before our first trip to the Balkans, I had a decent instrument to play.

In 2018, as we walked through the Holocaust Museum in Skopje, ouds and mandolins were everywhere. Photographs of Jewish mandolin orchestras from the 1920s and '30s, as well as pictures of youth groups playing those instruments while out on picnics dominated a few exhibits. Stencils of ouds decorated the walls as you walked through the museum. I remember that there was even a picture with an instrument that looked like an oud converted into a bass mandolin.

After we left Macedonia, our next stop was Thessaloniki in northern Greece. In the ten years after it became part of Greece as a result of the Balkan Wars, there was a huge displacement of the Turkish and Jewish populations, as well as a corresponding influx of Greeks. The forced movement of Greeks and Turks in the region is euphemistically called "the exchange of populations." What a nice term for the uprooting and murder of people who lived in those communities for centuries.

Tasos Theodorakis, another talented luthier who specializes in ouds, descends from Greeks displaced from Turkish Thrace and resettled in Thessaloniki. David Rapkievian plays one of Tasos's ouds and asked me to make sure to visit him. We had a very enjoyable visit at Tasos's atelier, or studio. There's a workbench in the back and instruments, with comfortable chairs, in the front. It's a space designed to promote drinking coffee (or something else) and playing music. We talked about our favorite oud players. His was Ara Dinkjian, a name I knew from my Armenian friend

Bitolan Jewish Mandolin Orchestra, 1920s. (Courtesy of United States Holocaust Memorial Museum)

Carolyn Rapkievian, but I really hadn't listened to his work. I promised Tasos I'd do so when I got home.

After a little bit of conversation, we discovered that Tasos's grandfather and my grandmother came from towns less than 25 miles apart in Thrace. Tasos handed me an oud from the 1930s with a new soundboard to play. Awkward, nervous, and then embarrassed, I barely plunked away at it, but then he opened the trap door to the basement. He gave me a tour of his shop, and we really hit it off. Although we didn't share a lot of vocabulary, we shared the language of builders. Tasos went through the whole process of how he built ouds. He even showed me part of his historic collection of instruments. I came to realize that he is as much an historian as a luthier, and he's a very nice man.

A few weeks after we returned home from that first Balkan trip, the Smithsonian Institution held its annual Folklife Festival. That year it featured Armenia, and my friend Carolyn helped coordinate the dance and music. One of the performers being celebrated was Onnik Dinkjian, a beloved 87-year-old singer whose lifetime of work has helped preserve the local Armenian dialect from Dikranagerd, which is now Diyarbekir, Turkey. Onnik was being backed up by his son Ara, Tasos's favorite oud player. Ara brought his latest group, The Secret Trio. A series of performances were scheduled. The first event was a concert by Onnik and the musicians at the Library of Congress's Coolidge Auditorium. My friend, Carolyn, was going to be the "MC." Waiting in the hallway for the doors to open, everybody talked about how Onnik sang at their parents' wedding, their wedding, and their children's weddings. They reminisced about how they saw him perform in Massachusetts, New Jersey, and even Maryland. I felt like I was going to see the "Armenian Frank Sinatra," and it seemed I would be the only non-Armenian in the crowd.

It was a great concert. Honestly, one of the best I've ever seen. Onnik, the crowd, and the other musicians had so much fun. I even sang along, without speaking a word of Armenian. The musicians keyed into Onnik. So clearly honoring him, you could see in their eyes that they wanted their performances to make him proud. On the way out, I bought almost every CD they had for sale and vowed to see the rest of their performances during the festival.

The next performance of Ara and The Secret Trio was outside. It was the beginning of July in Washington, DC. Onnik was letting the young guys perform without air conditioning. Thank goodness the humidity wasn't over ninety percent. With rugs and chairs set up, the small performance space in the Armenian exhibit of the festival more resembled a big outdoor living room than a stage. I got there early and saw Ara, a small, balding, middle-aged guy like me, come in with his oud on his back. Along with him were his band mates, Tamir, the kanun player, and Ismail, the clarinetist. They came early to grab lunch before the show.

Boldly, I introduced myself as a friend of Carolyn's, and told them how their concert with Onnik impressed me, especially about how they focused on him, and how they seemed like his kids trying to impress him. Ara looked at me and said, "You got it. You understood." I then bought the group baklava for dessert. We chatted a bit, and I found out that Ismail was originally from Bitola, while Tamir is from Turkey. These guys represented so many of the cultures that surrounded my grandfather when he was a boy in Monastir. Again, their concert was amazing. I remember coming home and telling my wife, Jessica, how much I enjoyed it, and somehow, how I felt connected to the music.

The last Secret Trio concert I saw was also outdoors (so, no Onnik), but it was on the main festival stage with the US Capitol as background and the Washington Monument in front of them. On the lawn were hundreds of people, mostly Armenians. I got a seat right up front. As at the Library of Congress, the people around me all shared connections to Ara and his father's music. When the music started, it was clear that everybody came to dance. Joy flowed from one person to another, from musicians to dancers and back.

I left thinking that these were Armenians, not Sephardic Jews, but I felt so connected. It sounds corny, but I really did feel something "stir inside of me." The trip to the Balkans broke free a piece of me relating to my Sephardic heritage and history. The previous week's performances connected with that piece. What was it about the music? The oud certainly resonated with me, but it was more than the music. It was the dancing. It was the language. All from people who were mostly descended from survivors of another genocide. The Armenians have the right to hold a grudge and be grim. Yet, they were so joyful. What was it that they carried in them? The music? The dance? The language? What was it that I could carry within me?

I started looking for Jewish oud players wanting to find out, "What was my music?" Back in Ottoman times, people like Haim Effendi, a player from Salonica recorded in both Turkish and Ladino. In more modern times, I found the recordings of Joe Elias and the Elias Ladino Ensemble. Right after World War Two ended, my Aunt Annie married Abe Elias. Maybe there was a connection?

My Uncle Abe came from a family of well-known Monastirli rabbis. He survived World War Two in the Pacific and been a union organizer for the International Lady Garment Workers Union. Music wasn't something I ever associated with him, but Annie certainly loved it. My dad tells stories of her listening to Saturday broadcasts of the Metropolitan Opera while taking her bath. Being the oldest, Annie had the best command of Ladino, one of the three languages my grandparents shared, and the one they used the most. When they wanted to tell secrets, they switched to Turkish. That worked until Annie started learning Turkish! I felt my family's music and language drawing me in, maybe somebody was trying to tell me some secrets? I needed to figure it out.

Building My Oud

My brain works most clearly and creatively while my hands build something out of wood. By training, I'm a carpenter and wooden boat builder. I spent 18 years running a community-based boatbuilding program in Alexandria, Virginia. Our apprentice program worked with kids about to be abandoned by "the system." We prepared them to lead decent lives and be good citizens. We also ran community and educational boatbuilding programs with any group that could benefit from the experience. Since then, I've helped other small boat groups and the Carpenter's Union develop hands-on math and pre-apprenticeship programs.

Contradictorily, my most powerful time in a shop I rarely get to experience. I'm usually teaching with a shop full of people. Yet, I've always done my best thinking when I'm alone working on a challenging project. My hands and a piece of my brain know what to do with the wood and tools. The rest of my brain frees up and thinks in a more associative way. It happens in a shop like nowhere else. And, if I make the time to write down my thoughts as they come, the experience gains tremendous personal value.

A year after our 2018 trip to the Balkans and Rante's initial research, a lot of family information needed processing. Through many coincidences, we knew our last name, and discovered lost family members. My thoughts about all this were jumbled and confused. I needed to see if I could straighten them out, identify what was bothering me, and determine why. I'm a builder, whether it's been on houses, boats, musical instruments, or young people. I decide what I want to make, draw up a plan, then build. I also love history, so my plan usually involves research. I wanted to try and figure out what I was really thinking about all I was uncovering. During the winter of 2019, I freed up much of my time between Thanksgiving and New Year's and decided to build an oud and think.

The Design

My view of my family broadened and opened with new questions as I learned more. The part of the family that stayed in Monastir wasn't ever talked about, beyond Jacob—"Poppa Grande." I realized I not only learned stories from my father, I also inherited his attitudes towards the people and places. I needed to puzzle this out and figure what it all meant to me. Why was I so interested?

I wanted to build an oud in a style which my grandfather, or great grandfather, would have heard and maybe even played. I learned there are two basic styles of ouds, Turkish and Arabic. The most famous of the Turkish style were made by a man called "Manol," while the most coveted Arabic ouds were made by the Nahant family. I figured that an instrument in circa 1900 Monastir would have been in the Turkish style. I started talking to people and gathering more information.

David Rapkivian confirmed my assumption that Jacob and Victor likely saw and heard Turkish ouds. He suggested I get back in touch with the oud builders I already knew, Tasos in Thessaloniki and Chris in Lowell. David also said I should call Ara Dinkjian. Few people knew more about that style and time period. David put Carolyn on the phone, and she gave me Ara's number.

I called. Ara was enthusiastic, saying it sounded like a "great project." I then broke his ear for 20 minutes. The whole story of my family and the trip poured out. A real gentleman, Ara graciously listened to it all and then told me I wanted to build a Turkish oud. To his knowledge there wasn't a specific Macedonian style. The ouds played in Monastir were brought in from elsewhere.

Ara offered to connect me with oud builders in Greece and Turkey knowledgeable about the oud styles available in 1900 Macedonia. He said Tasos was the man who would know the most. Ara also said Manol was the "Stradivarius" of ouds and that Tasos knew all about Manol. Recently, Ara recorded an album using a Manol oud, and Tasos wrote a biography about Manol for the liner notes. Soon after, I ordered that CD, *Conversations with Manol*, from Ara. He very generously threw in a bunch of cassettes for me to play in the tape deck of my '83 Benz. Several were of his dad, Onnik. When I told Jessica about this, she said that I was meeting so many nice people doing this project. I remember thinking about the types of people there are in the world. Oudists and Fascists are such a contrast.

Continuing my research, I wrote Tasos and decided to reach out to John Vergara, who owns the Lord of the Strings shop in Beacon, New York. I found John on the web—he seemed to be very well regarded—and Beacon is only about an hour up the Hudson River from my dad's house.

Following up on David Rapkevian's other suggestion, I called Chris Pantezelos in Lowell. Tremendously helpful and humorous, as always, he said, "Yes, the style that would have been in Monastir would be Turkish or Greek, and Manol was the best design." Chris happened to have a Manol on the bench which he would measure and document for me. He gave me the general set of measurements and promised more specifics. I was already building the oud in my head, just as I would a boat, thinking about drawing it full size, cutting sections through its shape, and then making patterns of all the parts.

I thought if I could find a Jewish oud player, would they maybe have some insight on the correct instrument design? Following my only lead on contemporary Jewish oud music, I looked up Joe Elias and the Elias Ladino Ensemble. I learned Joe was my Uncle Abe's first cousin. The Eliases were from Monastir, just like the Youchas. Joe passed away about 10 years earlier in 2010. His son, Dan, keeps the group and the music it preserved. I emailed Dan, and he confirmed that a Turkish style would have been used in Monastir.

Two weeks later (August 2019), I visited my dad. I took part of a day out of the visit to meet John Veranga in Beacon. Very generous with his time, he talked to me about specifics and construction details and let me photograph examples. Most importantly, he let me photograph his page of measurements for all the significant Ottoman ouds he has repaired or studied, including two Manols owned by Ara. The coincidences began to pile up, again. John's measurements, along with Chris's counsel and details, provided the foundation of my design work. From John, I also bought a big broken oud made in Izmir, Turkey. Far from a Manol, it gave me a physical example of how a Turkish oud went together. I figured I'd fix the instrument and give it to Emma. The family of Emma's Ladino teacher, Gloria Ascher, comes from Izmir. I thought there might eventually be a connection. (Which there was. Gloria now has the repaired oud in a place of honor in her living room.)

During that trip to my dad's, I spent a lot of time with him rebuilding his kitchen table. Building things together always has been a great way for us to interact. Jess commented that you'd think my dad would know that doing a project is when I communicate well. I've found the same thing with my kids—some of our best times together have been in the shop. It's how my brain works—along with my hands. It was why I wanted to build the oud.

After finishing the table, my dad and I sat in the dining room talking. He casually mentioned that during his childhood Aunt Annie and Grandma always played the mandolin. It floored me. Previously when I asked him if there was any music in the house when he was growing up, he just mentioned Annie listening to opera. I never heard of instruments being played in the family before—except for him playing the harmonica.

An aside about my dad and the harmonica… An intuitive player, he doesn't think, he just plays. The story of how he learned harmonica gives a little window into a piece of the man. My dad learned the instrument all on his own. His mom would not pay for piano lessons. Uncle Jack, who was older, took the money she gave him for lessons, saved it up, and rented a horse and cart to sell watermelons. After that, Grandma was done with paying for music lessons. My dad learned how to play harmonica on an instrument he bought himself. He told me,

> I started saving my pennies when I was about 7 years old, and by the time I was 8, I had my first harmonica. It was the height of the Depression, and my mother watched every cent. If I wanted any money I went out and shined shoes. I then gave [the money] to my mother who gave me an allowance of about a nickel a week—which was a lot in those days. It was the cost of a subway, or a cuppa coffee, or several ice cream cones.

Growing up, I heard my dad play the harmonica a lot, especially on camping trips. It was the entertainment. About 10 years ago, he broke the instrument he played my whole life. He bought another and was going to throw the old one out. Instead, I fixed it. It was metal work, but fittingly, it may have been the first instrument I repaired.

Aunt Annie is at the bottom right, next to the conductor. Members of the ILGWU Local 148 Mandolin Orchestra with their instruments at Union City, NJ, September 1934. (5780PB9F22L, Kheel Center, Cornell University)

Now, back to the conversation around the dining room table and mandolins... My dad said that Grandma and Annie took lessons as part of the International Lady Garment Workers Union (ILGWU) mandolin orchestra. Two minutes of searching on the Internet brought up a picture from 1934 of the local 148 mandolin orchestra from Union City. Aunt Annie is in the lower right. She must be 18 or 19. Annie looks just like the family photo taken a few years later when my dad was 10 and Annie was 21. This was about when my dad started learning the harmonica. He has no memory of ever wanting to play the mandolin, but I began to see more family connection to the oud and its descendants.

A couple of weeks later, (September 2, 2019) I heard from Tasos. He confirmed the popularity of Manol's style in Macedonia. I then asked him for some soundboard details. He said he showed me everything when I visited. I was sure he was right, but I didn't write it down! Looking back on my notes from the trip, I realized I only wrote about Jacob Ishach after we visited Bitola. Happily, I later remembered the details of how to attach the soundboard to the body. It was very, very helpful when the time came.

The next week (September 10), my Aunt Beck died. In the previous few months. I never got through when I tried calling her to check in and give updates on the family stories. Now, my dad was the last of his generation in the family. I remember thinking I'd better hurry up with my oud building.

By the beginning of November, I'd drawn a plan of my oud. A lot of the drafting tools I used came from Bill Hunley, my friend, the former Chief Naval Architect of the US Navy. His older coworkers and mentors gave them to him. He gave them to me. These drafting tools drew the 16-inch guns on the World War Two battleships. Now, they drew my oud. What a strange life for them! Bill wanted to see the drawings as soon as I was done. I was also figuring out that some of the wood would come from the stock Bill gave me.

Picking the wood for the instrument was an enjoyable, meaningful task. Through over 40 years of woodworking, I've acquired an interesting collection. Almost every piece comes with a memory, usually a memory of a good friend, or my family. The ebony for the fingerboard and maple for filler strips in the body came from Bill. Walnut and mulberry that I'd sawn from the tree would be alternating staves of the body. The walnut came from a friend's yard. I'd cut and milled it with another friend. The mulberry was from my folks' house. I ate its berries as a kid. The top came from spruce David Rapkievian salvaged from a piano that someone dumped in the Chesapeake and Ohio Canal outside of Washington, DC. And, I got to use sassafras for the head and tail blocks that my best friend from high school, Mikey, and I harvested from his yard. Mikey was a musical guy who pushed me to help my kids pursue their musical interests—something for which I'll be forever grateful. If I did my job right, the instrument was going to be beautiful.

As I drew and built the instrument in my head, I started thinking about how to bring more beauty out of my family's experience. I thought about the people I've known who have done so. In particular, I thought a lot about Sophiline Cheam Shapiro. As a young girl, Sophiline survived the Killing Fields of Cambodia. Her family was decimated. I believe her uncle was her only surviving male relative. During that genocide, the traditional court dancers were targeted. Only about a dozen survived, carrying in their minds and bodies hundreds of years of dance and choreography. After the overthrow of Pol Pot, the dancers immediately started teaching the next generation. Sophiline was one of their first students. She went on to become a world-famous dancer and choreographer. She stayed true to the traditions she learned, but she also combined those traditions with western themes, such as Othello, to tell the story of the Khmer Rouge. Her lessons are taught through beauty. She spent her life making sure her grandchildren will know her experiences—or at least a flavor, or an interpretation, of them. She's taking beauty out of absolute horror and leaving a legacy that my grandfather and great grandfather couldn't leave. Something I wish they had.

I thought that maybe part of what I was doing was trying to connect to my grandfather and his father. I didn't know much about them, but somehow, they seemed to be among my most influential relatives. It also hit me that building an oud combines two, or more, major themes of my life. The first theme was building and all the related connections: boats, craftsmanship, tools, and my teachers, like Bill. The second theme was family history. Something that always has loomed in the background, but recently has become an important piece of the puzzle. It was obvious, but maybe I was trying to leave a record of facts and relationships to lessen the mystery for a future researcher. The building process was certainly doing its job and stirring up my brain.

Drawing the oud took me back to the early days building boats at the Alexandria Seaport Foundation. We'd take xeroxed copies of boat plans from old books, combine them with volunteer labor and help from the kids in the community, and turn out some beautiful boats. It was a kick. Piecing the oud drawing together from the different sets of measurements and pictures took me back 20 years.

By the time I took the drawings up to Bill Hunley, he was pretty much bed bound. His body and parts of his memory were failing him, but his building brain was still sharp. He liked my drawings and wanted to see the oud as I progressed. I hoped I'd get to play it for him.

Design Details

Manol style ouds have elaborate rosettes, which decorate the insides of their three sound holes. My rosettes were going to be the major visible theme of the instrument. I wanted their design to reflect my family heritage and thought about incorporating the six petaled flower designs we'd seen on tombstones in Monastir's cemetery, as well as some form of our name. As a first step, I figured out the Hebrew spelling of Ishach, mainly from a Facebook page that my cousin Emily sent me. I found what those letters looked like in Rashi—the Hebrew typeface used by Sephardic Jews—and I copied them on Mylar. Emma developed a design for the larger, center sound hole which I really liked. Using the design in the instrument made another connection between family generations. Later, the design for the inlaid borders that surround the three rosettes came together. Cutting slices of multiple Stars of David and laying them alongside one another creates the pattern of triangles which I used around the sound holes and along the edge of the oud. All those small pieces of wood again came from friends. The dark wood was ron ron from the Trostles, dear friends of my parents, living in Costa Rica. The contrasting light wood was Bill Hunley's maple.

On my next trip to my dad's for his 92nd birthday, I stopped in New York and visited a Manol oud in the collection of the Metropolitan Museum of Art, the Met. The musical instruments are above the armor exhibit, which was my favorite as a kid. The oud sits right next to guitars by Jimmy D'Aquisto, John Monteleone, and John D'Angellico. Seeing their guitars at the Met's Guitar Heroes exhibit several years earlier really accelerated my building instruments with the kids and, by extension, building this instrument.

I had questions for the Met's "Manol" oud. I needed a whole list of information, including top, fingerboard and pegbox details. Even though I could only look and not touch, I took four pages of notes while studying that oud. When I got home, I really started assembling my instrument. The mold was already done. Now, I bent and glued in the ribs, made the top and prepared the stock for the rosettes and all the inlay that would go into the instrument.

I gathered building techniques from talking to generous luthiers, but I also relied on The Guild of American Luthiers, a very valuable organization. The culture of sharing embodied in their publications and conventions made my work so much easier. Thank God for Eugene Clark, a spectacular guitar builder who passed away a few years before I started the oud. Fortunately, he left some of his knowledge behind through the Guild. I read everything by him and about him I could find. His practical techniques for precise cutting and French polishing fit my way of working.

Around this time, I remember taking a picture of my workbench. It really said it all about how I work. Along with being a mess, the picture showed a cross section of my life. There were tools given to me by my mother, mother-in-law, and friends. The woods were from friends and family. I was using clamping and layout tricks from boat building and patterning tricks from fitting kitchen countertops. My past experiences, my family history, and my friends were all being incorporated into this instrument. As I worked, I wondered what, if anything, beyond the personal introspection, was going to come out of it.

My Dad Listening to Ara

"What is this music? It seems to come from the soul." Visiting for Thanksgiving, he sat at the kitchen table for breakfast while I worked on the oud at its other end and listened to Ara Dinkjian's CD, *Conversations with Manol*. My dad liked the music and asked about it. I explained how Ara recorded the solo piece the first time he played a particular oud built by Manol. The recording was as Ara played it, the same song order, basically untouched. "It comes from his soul. It's beautiful," my dad said.

Thrilled that he was now interested, I explained some about Ara's history, his music, and that the measurements for the instrument that I was building came from another Manol oud he owned. I then played some music by Ara's group that he has with Tamir and Ismail, The Secret Trio. When Ismail's clarinet led off a song, my dad said, "Listen to that cry. What pain." When the group really started rocking, my dad said that it reminded him of the music Betty Turner (a cousin) danced to at Esther Negrin's wedding. (Esther was another cousin on his father's side.) The women took over and danced on the tables. The men stuck money in their clothes. My dad thinks he was around five. It obviously made an impression.

I explained that Ismail was from Bitola, and we talked about the universality of the music—how it was shared by the different cultures that mixed in the area—Turkish, Armenian, Greek, Roma, and Jewish. My dad wanted to know more about Ara. I showed him the interview my friend, Carolyn Rapkivien, did with Ara and his father Onnik when they performed at the Library of Congress and the Folklife Festival. In the interview, Onnik and Ara explain their family's origins from Dikranagerd in the Ottoman empire. They talk about how after the Armenian Genocide Onnik was born in Paris, orphaned, and then moved to the US. They also told the story of how, on a visit to Paris when Ara was 18, they talked to an old woman who was probably the only person alive that remembered that Onnik's father played the oud.

"This could be our family." My dad had tears in his eyes. Again, I explained the universality of our family's experience. How the research into the family was discovering and uncovering facts that we didn't know before—or had lost.

Before that morning, I tried several times to lay out for my dad what we experienced on our trip and subsequently found out. He just hadn't seemed interested. A year earlier, when I was showing him pictures from our trip, he stood up and walked out of the room. Now sitting at the kitchen table, he was asking related questions. So, I tried again.

"How come you never told me this?" my dad asked. I was dumbfounded and said that this was probably our sixth time through the story. He said I hadn't. Jessica backed me up, but it didn't matter. He was interested, and he was listening. I explained what we knew up to that point—about Jacob and his second family. Ara's music and his family story took down whatever barriers were inside my father's head. A wall had been breached. I don't know what that wall was, or why it was there, but the music of a similar culture, and the story of a similar family broke through.

Thinking While Building

As I planked up the body of the oud, the building process certainly made me think. I realized the instrument really was an oud of history, or stories—stories about my friends and family told through wood and tools, as well as the history of my family and the Sephardic Jews of Ottoman Macedonia.

I kept reading histories about the Jews of the Balkans. It was a vibrant culture for a long time. Reading about its destruction was so sad. I spent a fair amount of time wondering what positive or useful lesson you can take away from such an incomprehensible event as the mass murder and destruction of a culture and its place.

I think it's all about minimizing hate between people. Hate kills. I'd spent years working in my community trying to lessen the hate between young people and the dominant world around them. I'd spent more years helping others do similar work, mostly through boat building and carpentry-related projects. About ten years after I started doing this type of work, I realized I did the work to honor a friend, Doug, who was killed during college. The young man who killed him was Black. He was flunking out of college. He set fire to the dorm hall and killed the first White person who tried to help him. It was my friend, Doug, who was just trying to get people out of a burning building. I never made the connection before between my family research and Doug. I guess everything leads to the same place.

During my reading, I ran across something that said Yehuda Halevi composed using Arabic *makams*, or musical patterns. One of the great Sephardic poets of medieval Spain, the Jewish liturgy still uses his poems and songs. I read Halevi's poems in college when I had the opportunity and privilege of studying with Professor Yosef Yerushalmi, one of the great contemporary Jewish scholars. As I was getting drawn into my family's story, I felt, again, how I must have disappointed Professor Yerushalmi. I certainly remember the look on his face when he tried to get me to work both harder and better. One of Professor Yerushalmi's most influential works is called *Zakhor*, "remember" in Hebrew. This short, dense book about historiography asks, "What do Jews chose to remember and how?" Thinking about Professor Yerushalmi made me realize I was puzzling out how to use this gift of family history that was being given to me.

By the end of the first week of December, I had the instrument popped off its mold and was inlaying the details into the top. I also put the label in. Many times, the builder of an oud places their picture on the instrument's label. The only self-portrait I've ever done is a woodcut print I did in a college art class. For some reason, I saved it. After scanning the print and using a computer program to mimic the oud's inlaid border, I put in my name, address, date along with "first oud based on family history" and glued the label to the inside of the instrument.

December 15th was the last official day of my "building and thinking" break. I figured two part-time weeks of work to go, and the oud would be together. New Year's was the new target. I didn't make it. More things interfered.

Ladino Day

On Sunday January 12, 2020, at the Sephardic Brotherhood's Ladino Day in New York, a lot came together. Emma participated in a youth panel talking about their experiences with Ladino and its meaning in their lives. Em's friend and Ladino teacher, Gloria Ascher, was presenting and

Dan Elias and the Elias Ladino Ensemble were playing. I was excited to meet Dan in person for the first time. Jess, my dad, and I all went.

We got up to New York Saturday night. My dad was asleep. It was great seeing Emma, who made me a painting of an oud! We stayed up late looking at bound copies of the *Little Review*, a 1920s literary magazine that published the writings of Israel Solon, my mom's father's best friend and my mom's intellectual mentor. The magazine represented the intellectual curiosity which Israel passed to her and she to her children and grandchildren. For me, it was a moving evening.

In the morning, Emma rehearsed their panel talk with Jessica while I talked to my dad. He asked me again why I'd become so interested in his side of the family versus Mom's side. For the first time I articulated the idea that Mom knew her family as rounded people and presented them to me that way. I was looking for context to round out his family from caricatures to characters.

My dad saw the accuracy of my description and said his way of relating to the family came from his mother. She pushed people away, especially the family. He did the same thing. I think he came to the realization that he's a combination of his mother and father—his caring father on the inside and his independent, pushing away mother on the outside. My dad felt it was a great insight. It was worth the trip, just for that conversation.

Ladino Day was eventful. We took a cab downtown to the Sephardic Federation building on W. 16th St. Walking in we saw Yaakov Bernstein, our 2018 Balkan "tour mate" who led us saying the Sephardic mourner's prayer in Bitola's cemetery. It was great seeing him. As people found their seats, Dan Elias and his group played some nice music. About to sit down, I saw Dave Bell standing in the aisle next to the stage. I'd known Dave for about 10 years. I nearly crushed my dad's feet getting over to him. Dave is a sailing ship captain, merchant mariner, and maritime educator, and I taught him how to teach hands-on math through boat building. I asked Dave what he was doing at Ladino Day. He said he came to see his cousin, pointing at Dan. He asked what I was doing there. I said I came to see my cousin, pointing at Dan. It turns out Dave and Dan are first cousins. Dave's mother and Dan's dad were brother and sister. They were first cousins to my Uncle Abie.

That's quite a coincidence. There aren't a lot of Jews teaching with small boats and building cigar box guitars. We also both wrote teaching books for kids. Why were two descendants from the mountain town of Monastir doing this work? That puzzling connections still makes me smile. Dan's concert was great. I didn't grow up listening to much Sephardic music, but I thought I recognized the song "Avram Avinu" from my early childhood. There was no solid memory, but it certainly sounded very familiar.

The Sephardic world is incredibly small, and there were connections being made all over the place that day. Emma's teacher Gloria talked about teaching Ladino. She was great, very funny, passionate, and sincere. She's taught over 600 students and loved every second. It's amazing she grew up just hearing the language and not speaking it. The daughter of the woman who convinced Gloria to teach Ladino sat in front of us. Her mother was a famous poet. When Dave came over to talk wearing his "Tienes raki?" t-shirt, he mentioned speaking a few words of Serbo-Croat when he visited Bitola in the 1980s. An officer on a ship that stopped in Greece, he took a taxi up to the mountains. Dave's mention of Serbo-Croat engaged the lady next to us. It was Betty Jagoda, the daughter of Flory Jagoda the well-known Sephardic singer. We made the connection to Susan Gaeta, Flory's musical apprentice who has become a friend and whose group, Trio Sephardi, I've seen several times.

Emma's panel of three young people gave a hopeful perspective for the future of Ladino. Emma was very thoughtful and well spoken. A young man from Los Angeles seemed to have made Ladino his cause. The third young person, Janice, grew up writing letters in Ladino to her grandfather in Istanbul. They used the nearly extinct Solitreo script as their own secret language. Her grandfather must have been quite a guy. I hope she realizes how lucky she is.

A professor from SUNY Binghamton, Brian Kirschen, talked about Izmir, and Sarah Aroeste sang. Sarah is probably the best known Monastirli/American performer. She writes and performs original materials in Ladino, using a wide range of musical styles. She and Dan's group closed the afternoon with "Adio Kerida," probably the most popular Sephardic song.

Then, an old family friend, Naomi Kleinberg, showed up! Even though I'd known her my whole life, I never realized that she had Sephardic heritage. When Naomi was a young woman, my mom helped steer her into books and editing. They were working on projects almost until my mom passed away seven years earlier. Naomi made Emma cry talking about my mom and how she would talk about how much she loved her grandkids. She certainly did, and they her.

Before the event started, all the presenters spent a few hours together. Dan now called Emma "Primo," "cousin" in Ladino. Dan gave us copies of the CD he did with his dad. And he said his mom had ten of his dad's ouds in the basement. He was trying to sell them to a traditional music store in Maryland. I told him I'd love to see them first. It also turned out Aunt Annie and Dave and Dan's aunt, Mary Camhi, were good friends. I remember hearing Mary's name, but I don't remember the context.

A couple of days after the event, Emma sent me an article from the Jewish *Forward* about Ladino Day. Emma is really featured. And the writer mentions an old man sitting behind her that kept up a running commentary and just smiled and nodded when the writer turned and tried to shush him. The old man was my dad. The following week Joseph Benatov sent a link from a Sephardic publication where Emma was all over the pictures. There was also a picture of the *Forward* writer and my dad in the row behind her.

Finishing the Oud

Zack celebrated his 21st birthday on MLK Day. It seemed like an ideal day to finish the oud. I strung it up and played Zack "Happy Birthday." Jess videoed it and texted it to him. I didn't play very well, but it was fun to do. That morning our local Pacifica radio station played recordings of Dr. King's speeches. The commentator talked about how racism was fear of people that the racists didn't know—people they didn't see in their everyday lives and didn't talk to. That hasn't changed.

Over the next week, I took the oud to David Rapkievian in Maryland and up to Bill Hunley in Waterford, Virginia. David played the instrument and made it sound good. It was very gratifying. When I played the instrument that night there was a moment when it felt great—warm and resonant—like it really holds pieces of my friends and family.

When I took the oud out to Bill Hunley, he really liked it. I got to play him a song, which made both of us smile. There's a lot of his wood in the instrument. That's probably why it feels so warm. Both Zack and Emma called while I was at Bill's and got to talk to him. I think it was the last time they spoke.

My oud. (Joe Youcha photo)

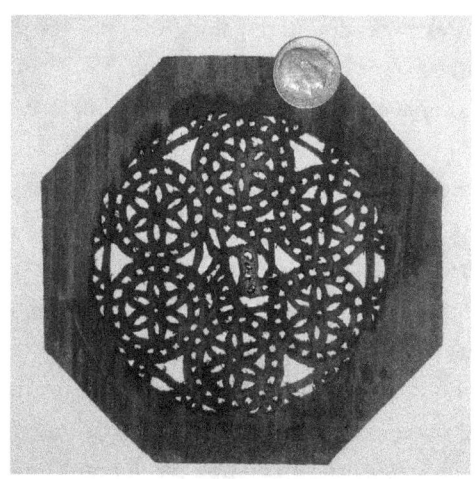

Soundhole rosette. Over 200 cuts. (Joe Youcha photo)

It all made me think about my dad's "link in the chain" metaphor. At Ladino Day, there were three generational links of our family. I'd been looking backwards to get context about earlier links. Emma, I thought, was looking forward. It will be interesting to see how Emma pursues things. I realized I was also starting to look forward. I felt I couldn't see the destination, but I was starting to see the next few possible steps on the path.

Ladino

"You're Jewish? You don't speak Jewish?" I can still hear my Aunt Annie and Aunt Beck describing how it was for them visiting Jewish friends growing up in 1930s New York. They'd be asked by their friends' parents how they could be Jewish if they didn't speak Yiddish. Yiddish, derived from Old German, is the language of northern European Jews, Ashkenazi Jews. It's not the language of my father's family. We are Sephardic Jews. We come from "Sepherad," Spain's Hebrew name. Talking with other Sephardic families, I've heard stories similar to my aunts' many times.

When expelled from Spain in 1492, Sephardic Jews brought the Ottoman Empire technology, trade, and culture. We also brought our language, "Ladino," "Judeo-Espanyol," "Judezmo"—call it what you like. Written in Hebrew letters, it's essentially 15th century Castilian Spanish with added words from the different cultures we encountered along the way. Even though my father was born on the Lower East Side of Manhattan in 1925, it's his first language. I have clear images of him sitting at the dining room table with several books spread out around him, reading aloud to himself. The books were written with Hebrew letters, but the language my father was speaking was essentially Spanish, Ladino.

As a kid, I studied French. The language my mother loved. I never learned Ladino, or Spanish. Maybe it was a sign of rebellion against my father. French has been useful, especially doing this research, but I've always felt like the guilty link who broke the chain. My family likely spoke some sort of Spanish once the language evolved from Latin about a thousand years ago. I tried learning Spanish or Ladino several times, and always thought the language in our family would end with my father. I failed to account for my children and their cousins.

Both my kids, Emma and Zack, took Spanish in school and are conversant in the language, as is my niece, Lisa. It's really been Emma's interest in Ladino that sparked a good part of this research journey. During the last year of college, Emma started studying Ladino with Gloria Ascher. There's almost a 60-year difference between them, but Emma and Gloria are good friends and talk, in Ladino, almost every week. It's touching to watch, but there's still an itch inside of me. I should also know the language—or at least more of it than I do.

As mentioned earlier, family stories have my grandfather Victor speaking between eight and eleven languages. Ladino was only his first. In fact, he had to relearn Ladino in order to court my grandmother. I

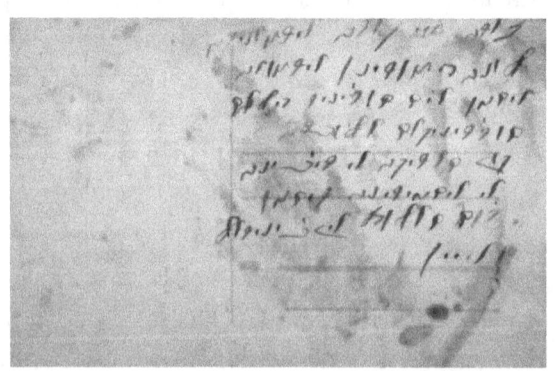

A postcard from Bitola written in Ladino using the Solitroe script. (Courtesy of the Archives of the Alliance Israélite Universelle)

wondered how my grandfather could speak so many languages. I learned he studied them in school.

The Alliance

"The Alliance." I've heard those words all my life said with a tone of reverence for the French-run Jewish school network that educated my grandfather. Somehow, a Jewish boy from the mountains of Monastir got a good French education in Tunisia. Since it's a story I grew up with, I never thought it was odd, only adventurous. Until I was much older, running a type of educational organization myself, I never realized the organizational challenges involved.

Founded in 1860 by a group of French Jews, the *Alliance Israelite Universelle* (AIU) based itself on the ideals of the Jewish Enlightenment (*Haskalah*). Most influential from 1880 until the Balkan Wars, World War One, and the subsequent fall of the Ottoman Empire, the organization focused on "raising up" Jews mainly from around the Mediterranean in the Ottoman Empire and North Africa. Many of these Jews were horribly poor, uneducated, and superstitious, with limited career opportunities. Through their schools, the Alliance wanted to train them to become good, productive citizens of their countries—just like the Jews were in France.

Narcisse Leven was at the center of the Alliance from its beginning. In 1911, Leven, by then a Senator of France, wrote the 50-year history of the organization. He described how its work was primarily done through a network of over one hundred schools. In order to receive Alliance support, these schools needed local support. If the AIU decided to place a school in a community, it was usually after the community started and ran for several years a school modeled on the AIU. Once an AIU school started, everything ran through the Central Committee in Paris: finances, staffing, facilities, and curriculum. Most schools served students from the local communities. There were, however, several schools that served all the communities within the Alliance's network. Around 1900, these included two agricultural schools, the one in Tunisia where my grandfather went and another one in Palestine. There was also a technical school in Jerusalem and a normal school in Paris used to train teachers. The

Alliance believed very strongly that it should recruit its teachers from its graduates.

The Alliance didn't exist in a vacuum. It was one of many efforts by wealthy Western Jews to "help" their poorer "Oriental" brethren. A German Jew who made a fortune building railroads throughout the Ottoman Empire, Baron Maurice De Hirsh, funded several of these efforts. Two of the organizations financed by the Baron, the Alliance and the Jewish Colonization Association (JCA), were largely run by Narcisse Leven who for many years served as president of both. The organizations believed strongly in getting the targeted Jews out of their traditional commerce-based livelihoods, and giving them the knowledge, apprenticeships, and tools to become farmers, professionals, and tradesmen. Interestingly, both the Alliance and the JCA were anti-Zionist. They believed that the Jewish farmers should become productive members of their surrounding nation and not start a nation of their own.

As mentioned earlier, the Alliance's organization was very centralized, very French. It ran on paper and left an extensive archive in Paris. The existence of these records is a minor miracle. Most of them were taken by the Nazis in World War Two as exhibits for a museum to document the extinct Jewish race. After the German defeat, the Alliance was able to reclaim most of the records, although some got "lost." It turns out they weren't lost; the Soviets took them. The "lost" portion was finally returned to Paris by Russia in 2001.

I thought I knew all I needed to know about the Alliance as far as it concerned my family. It seemed a dead end. My cousin Emily sent me her mom Linda's correspondence with the archive in Paris. Looking through their materials, the Alliance archivists found no mention of my grandfather's name in any of their indexes. There might be some mention of him in the correspondence between the Farm School in Tunisia and the Central Committee in Paris, but since we didn't know the exact year, it would mean reading through thousands of pages of correspondence.

While building my oud, I decided to look further. There's a tremendous amount of materials online. A major question for me was whether my French, after 40 years of inactivity, would be up to the task. (It was. Barely.) I started with the Alliance's annual Bulletins. These reports summarize the yearly activities of the organization, its local committees, and schools, as well as issues important to the community. An Alliance Bulletin provided Mark Cohen with the account of Jacob Samuel Ishach being beaten in a village as part of a blood libel.

I searched for Jacob's name in the Bulletins' list of the local committee members. As a supposedly prominent person, maybe he would be a member? I struck out. Next, I looked for mention of my grandfather, Victor. I had better luck, but nothing truly solid. In the Djédéida, Tunisia Farm School's summary report from 1907, on page 148, it says that four students left to work on farms in Canada. And, on pages 149 and 150, the Bulletin tells the story of the hardships these students encountered in Canada. In particular, the author referenced a letter from B. Boccarra.

I knew from my cousins' research that when the *SS Liguria* arrived in New York on April 4, 1907, from Genoa, its passenger manifest listed Benjamin Bokara [Boccarra], Alberto Foa, Kaim [Haim] Youshah, and Mardoche Karan as workmen coming from Tunis, on their way to Montreal. The "friend" sponsoring them is "Ancell, President du Baron de Hirsch, Montreal, Canada." Discovering the new information in the Alliance Bulletin confirmed the family stories and motivated me to see if I could find more in the Alliance records.

Searching was a two-step process. I knew from my cousin Emily that a portion of the Alliance materials were available online through Harvard's library. They had digitized rolls of microfilm. Finding a document required first searching the online index of the Alliance Archives and then finding the correct digitized microfilm roll in Harvard's collection.

Narcisse Leven in about 1912. (Courtesy of the Archives of the Alliance Israélite Universelle)

I looked for information about both the Farm School in Djédéida and any Alliance schools in Monastir. Nothing came up using any of the variety of spellings for my family's last name. It was disappointing, but I noticed something. Harvard's collection listed no materials pertaining to the former Yugoslavia. Of all the information that interested me, these rolls seemed to be missing.

Harvard's archivist double-checked. And, yes, those rolls weren't there. She suggested I contact the Director of the Alliance Archives in Paris. In February of 2021, I reached out to Jean-Claude Kuperminc and laid out my situation, what I knew about my grandfather's interaction with the Alliance, and what I hoped to find. Director Kuperminc soon replied, "The case you refer to reminds me of our virtual exhibition on the Jews of Bitola," and he gave me a link to the exhibit's website. In all my Internet searches, I never saw the exhibit. It never came up. Obviously, I had not searched the Alliance's website well enough!

On the fourth slide of the online exhibit, I found my grandfather. On the sixth slide, I found reference to my great grandfather. I was, and still am, stunned by finding this information. Naturally, I immediately emailed Director Kuperminc and asked his help pursuing this lead. He thought I should talk to Emre Yarvuz, a young Turkish student who, as an intern in their library two years earlier, created the exhibit.

Monastir, Djédéida, and Canada 1903–1910

Victor In Monastir

When I first contacted Emre, he sent me a list of documents on his computer related to my grandfather, whom he called Haim Youchah. Emre found the documents in the AIU Archives during his master's thesis research. After finishing his degree in France, Emre moved back home to Istanbul. Since the Alliance hadn't yet digitized the documents from the former Yugoslavia, he needed to get copies of the documents from his friends at the archives in Paris for my research. I was so excited I couldn't wait. I dove into the correspondence and histories of the Alliance.

From Emre's virtual exhibit I knew my grandfather attended the Alliance school in Monastir, but there's no family story saying so. I honestly never thought about where my grandfather went to school as a boy before I started doing the family research. It turns out there were lots of schooling possibilities in Monastir for a young Jewish boy during the first decade of the 1900s. The town wasn't only a physical borderland battlefield in Ottoman Macedonia, but also a cultural and religious one. In Monastir, the Talmud Torah school educated Jewish boys in the traditional religious manner of drill and repetition. There were also Greek, Turkish, and Bulgarian educational institutions, American and English missionary efforts, a French Lazarist brother's school, as well as the Alliance's work with both boys and girls. And the Bulgarians, Turks, and Greeks were happy to send their teachers into any institution to teach language classes. These groups all fought for influence over the minds and souls of the resident young people. Monastir's Jews attended every one of these schools.

The Alliance's boys' school in Monastir was established in 1895. There had been a local Alliance committee and an Alliance-styled school in the town for about 20 years before the central committee in Paris decided to directly invest in the community. I knew this from reading the histories of the community. To learn more, I dug into Narcisse Leven's 50-year history of the Alliance. A French copy exists online. Enough of my French came back for me to make sense of the text with the help of an online dictionary and Google Translate.

I learned that Monastir had the second Alliance school in Ottoman Macedonia, behind Salonica in education, as it was in trade, religion, and culture. In 1895, Monastir was a town of 65,000 with about 6,000 Jews. Leven says, "The Jews of Monastir are very practical, very attached to their faith, their costumes, their customs. Five or six families are relatively rich, a hundred and fifty others are well off; the rest live hard [lives…they] speak Turkish, Greek, and Bulgarian as fluently as Judeo-Spanish, their mother tongue."

The Alliance provided both boys and girls with an education that was both "Jewish and modern." A separate girls' school opened in 1901. By 1913, there were 269 boys in school and 204 girls. The traditional Jewish school for boys, the Talmud Torah, continued with 290 students.

AIU records show that Victor started in Monastir's Alliance school 4 years before he went to Tunisia in 1903. This means he likely started in the fall of 1899. The Alliance school's founding Director, David Levy, described the 1899–1900 school year in his Annual Report. The school started the year with 293 students and ended with 246, (200 boys, 46 girls). The reasons for 38 leaving varied from going back to the Talmud Torah, attending Greek or Bulgarian schools, or moving from Monastir. Students also left when they were old enough to work. Levy says that some of the students went to the three-year business school in Salonica and were the most brilliant students. Equal numbers of paying and scholarship students attended the school in Monastir, but with the economic disparity between the two towns, most of the Monastirli paying students couldn't have afforded the same schooling in Salonica. Levy also talks about trying to engage the parents with monthly report cards. He says that no matter what they teach in school, morals and beliefs must also come from the home.

As with all their schools, the Alliance tried to provide a well-rounded education that would lead to the students' future success and enable them to remain tied to Judaism. In his report, Director Levy lays out how a student progressed through the school. In the first year they studied a piece of biblical history, or the "History of the Saints," along with postbiblical history, French grammar, French language, arithmetic, history, theoretical science, and practical science. In their second year, they continued all those subjects and added geography. In the third year, students studied biblical history, French grammar, French language, arithmetic, and general science lessons. The last three years focused on French, arithmetic, and general science lessons.

Local schools implemented the basic curriculum established in Paris, fitting it to meet their circumstances. The Central Committee also dictated that girls should learn sewing, and all students must learn the local language. In early 1900s Monastir, this language was Turkish. Director Levy's correspondence also indicates in different school years there were the aforementioned classes in Greek and Bulgarian languages taught by instructors provided by those communities. Reading the Alliance documents made it obvious how my grandfather learned so many languages.

Records show Victor received free clothes from the Alliance for several years. This wasn't unusual for Alliance students in Monastir, especially since a fire devastated the Jewish Quarter on July 25, 1897. This fire must have impacted the family. Even though Jacob was a *Mouktar*, he took the Alliance's help while evidently rebuilding the family's life and home.

Times were undoubtedly hard in Monastir. My father remembers Victor's pockmarked nose. We always assumed he contracted smallpox when he went to North Africa. It doesn't appear so. AIU records show a smallpox outbreak in Monastir in Spring 1896. It certainly hit the Jewish community. Director Lévy reported to the Central Committee in Paris that on the 10th of April 1896 one of school's students died of smallpox.

Victor probably contracted the disease at the same time. It doesn't appear he got it in Tunisia. The AIU correspondence between Tunisia and Paris from 1903 through 1907 shows no mention of smallpox. In most of those Director's reports, there's a section about the health of the students. The only epidemic mentioned is an outbreak of typhus in Tunis, whose spread the school was very careful to prevent.

Any knowledge of Victor's Alliance school career in Monastir was lost to the family before Emre recovered it in the institution's archives. The big family story we heard about Victor's youth in Monastir was that he witnessed a murder. As a result, his father sent him to the farm school outside of Tunis. Growing up outside of New York City in the 1960s and '70s, this seemed like a story straight out of *The Godfather*. What type of person would be killed where a young witness would need to leave the country for his own safety? I tried to think through the situation many times; it was a puzzle Emre solved.

Victor left Monastir in 1903, the year of the Illinden Uprising, when Macedonian revolutionaries tried to wrest their independence from the Ottoman Turks. On Saturday, May 9, 1903, the new Alliance Boy's School Director, M. David Arié, reported that three days earlier (Wednesday, May 6th) several Christians were murdered in front of the school during lunch break. The students all saw it happen. The school was closed for several days. Reading the report brings immediacy.

> I am pained to let you know that the school was closed Thursday and Friday, and we won't have students until tomorrow. All of Monastir is in an indescribable panic. Wednesday past, during lunch break, a few insurgent assassins threw [bombs] in front of the whole school population and me. Fathers and mothers of some of the students who were taking lunch in the heart of the building reclaimed their children in a panic. I took great pains to calm the parents of students who came later. Several minutes later the school was deserted. Everyone locked themselves in their homes awaiting with terror the events. The authorities sent guards for the whole day which ended without incident.

The next day we reopened the school with 3/4s of our students and things went peacefully until we had an alarm at 11 o'clock. I consulted with the scholarly committee [administrators and teachers] and sent the students home…

The school was closed from noon on Thursday through Friday. During this time the markets were closed, and everyone stayed home. On the streets, you didn't see anyone but guards and horse patrols. It's a true terror in the whole town. I will keep you up to date until we have a safe life.

It was a big deal. Through their surrogates, the major powers were all pushing against one another in Macedonia. The area was being watched closely. The murder my grandfather witnessed even made the *New York Times* on May 10, 1903. Under a headline reading "Casualties in Macedonia," there's a brief piece saying, "Thirteen Christians were killed and 19 wounded and 3 Musselmans [Muslims] were killed during the recent outbreak in Monastir."

This was all part of the preliminary violence leading up to the official outbreak of the Illinden Uprising that August. It must have been awful for my grandfather, his parents, and his baby sister, who lived through all of it. A summary of the Alliance correspondence really gives a good picture of the times, and the impact of events on the Jewish community.

May 20, 1903

Boy's school Director Arié writes the central committee describing the situation, saying that the community is dealing with Bulgarian anti-Semitism, but that some Jewish families were sheltering Greeks and Bulgars.

June 10, 1903

Arié doesn't want to send the Central Committee the names of the Jewish families sheltering the wounded and scared Bulgarians and Greeks. The Moslem authorities might misinterpret the families' actions. The Jews are between "the hammer and the anvil."

July 28, 1903
>   From Arié to Central Committee
>
>   "Bulgarians assassinated J. Benyakar and two Albanian Moslems in Crouchova—about a 12-hour march from Monastir. The lack of security has raised the pain one hundred percent among the Jewish families."

In the same letter we learn from M. Arié of Victor's application to go to the farm school in Tunisia. "I have the honor to include two applications for the Farm School at Djédéida. The two proposed students are in all points superior to the candidate for Mikevah (the school in Palestine.) I hope for this backward community of Monastir that my four candidates are accepted. The vilayet of Monastir is one of the most fertile in Turkey. It's very important that agricultural workers are prepared for the eventualities." Sadly, it seems that copies of the applications no longer exist in the Alliance Archives in Paris.

August 10, 1903 (Seven days after the official start of the uprising)
>   "Day to day, the situation in Monastir gets more critical. The bands of insurgents are more powerful and more numerous. They create havoc and burn entire villages, everything that is in their way. The garrison of Monastir is quintupled without effect. The new reinforcements arrive. We're assured that nothing bad will happen to the town. The waiting is killing our soul. I still want the school open to prevent the children from being in the streets and parks during the crisis."
>
>   "The assassination of [the Russian] Counsel didn't do anything to calm the general turmoil." Arié then tells the story of the assassination. The counsel slapped a Turkish soldier who didn't salute. The soldier then shot him.
>
>   "One thing is certain, the authorities are using all their power to upset the insurgents. At this moment, Monastir is isolated from the point of view of the telegraph. The Bulgarians keep cutting the telegraph lines. They've unsuccessfully tried to derail the train."
>
>   "A telegram signed by [the community] has asked the Sultan to put an end to this untenable situation."

The situation wasn't going to get much better. Between 1903 and 1908, approximately 8,000 people were murdered in Bitola and the surrounding area. It's easy to see why on September 20, 1903, Victor Youchah

May 9, 1903, report from Director Arié to the President of the Alliance documenting the attack held in front of the school. (Courtesy of the Archives of the Alliance Israélite Universelle)

left Monastir and started making his way to the Alliance farm school in Djédéida, Tunisia. He never returned to Macedonia.

Victor Goes to Tunisia

When he was 14, Victor left the cool mountains of Monastir for the heat of the North African Mediterranean coast. He didn't go alone. Another young man, Elie Graciani, accompanied him. Director Arié and the Alliance were smart enough to send two kids together. The exact route they traveled is unknown, although I think it's safe to assume they took a ship from Salonica. This meant an 8-hour ride on a train frequently bombed and derailed during the previous months. Did an adult accompany them to Salonica? The boys then caught a ship headed for Tunis. Perhaps they were able to find a ship going there directly? Perhaps, they changed ships in another Mediterranean port? I doubt we'll ever know those details. Through the report of the farm school's director, we know

1912 Alliance Boy's School 4th year students in alphabetical order. Victor is last, listed as "Haim Youcha." (Courtesy of the Archives of the Alliance Israélite Universelle)

that they were part of a class of eighteen students, and that they were the only "Turcs."

Started eight years before my grandfather arrived, the farm school was in Djédéida, a town "on the doorstep" of Tunis, only 25 kilometers from the center of the city. Good farming land with the river Medjerdah running through it, the school included a railroad station and a local village. I hope my grandfather and Elie Graciani were met at the boat in Tunis, rather than having to find their way to the train for Djédéida. Regardless, when they arrived at the farm school, Narcisse Leven, in his 50-year history of the Alliance, describes what they found:

> A large low plain, undulating from 1500 to 1550 hectares. The richest and most fertile lands are found on the banks of the Medjerdah; there are vines, olive trees, orchards, and plantings of shrubs. Along the Chafroun wadi are artificial meadows which serve as pasture for the herds. Farther on, and at a distance where the influence of the rivers is no longer felt, extend less rich lands, good, however, for great [vine] cultivation. Finally, the high parts of the hills serve as food for the sheep. Numerous wells, scattered throughout the property, provided an abundance of drinking water to the settlers and natives of the surroundings and were used to water the herds. When the estate was bought, it already had all the varied plantings required for the students' agricultural training, all the crops that are possible in Tunisia, [including] 7,000 olive trees occupying 113 hectares and which can be easily irrigated; 22 lots of vines in full yield, and fruit [orchards], various forest species, arable farming [on] over a thousand hectare [and] artificial grasslands.

This was quite a change from Monastir. The two boys came from a climate slightly warmer than Burlington, Vermont, to a climate slightly warmer than Albuquerque, New Mexico. It was also much drier in Tunisia. Monastir gets five times as much precipitation as Djédéida. And Djédéida was a healthy climate. Rarely is there any mention of an illness in the school director's reports. The school operated an olive oil mill, a flour mill, a forge, a cheese making plant, electrical generation, and later, a café. These facilities not only served to train the students, they earned income for the school.

The school in Djédéida wasn't the Alliance's first effort at training Jewish farmers. Twenty-five years earlier, the organization established the Mikevah Israel farm school located about a 45-minute walk from the city of Jaffa in Palestine. The driving force of the Alliance's effort was Charles Netter. During a trip to Palestine in 1868, he noted seeing "in Jerusalem only one Israelite working a piece of land." Netter's idea was that by becoming farmers the Jews of Palestine could raise themselves up from being small merchants or relying on the charity of Jews around the world. Previous unsuccessful attempts to train Jewish farmers in Palestine included one by Moses Montifiore, the great Jewish philanthropist. The Alliance eventually took over Montifiore's land.

This ideal of a noble Jewish farmer wasn't foreign to intellectual western European Jews. The Jewish enlightenment movement occurred in a few Western European countries and contained a strong "back to the land" element. Jews were historically forced into ghettos and petty commerce. If they could own and work land, or learn a trade, they would become contributing members of their countries. This would counteract the anti-Semitic stereotype of Jews being leeches on a Christian society. The Alliance's leadership decided to launch the farm school in Tunisia, largely to serve the Tunisian Jews whom the Alliance viewed as downtrodden by their urban existence and in need of learning an agrarian profession and lifestyle.

The job of starting the school was given to Samuel Avigdor. Originally from Andrianople (now Edirne on the Turkish border with Bulgaria) Avigdor attended the agricultural school in Montpellier, France, and served as an assistant director at the Alliance's farm school in Palestine. His reports make up the bulk of the Alliance correspondence relating to my grandfather's time at the Djédéida farm school. Reading Avigdor's letters to the Alliance's central committee reminds me of the reports I used to write to my Board of Directors when I ran the Alexandria Seaport Foundation (a much smaller bureaucracy). Our work was very similar—training disadvantaged youths in skills that would enable them to lead productive lives. Along the way, the organizations needed to generate enough revenue to cover a portion of the program's costs. I know from personal experience some of the pressures under which this man worked 120 years ago. I don't envy him.

In only eight years, the school in Djédéida grew from 20 to almost 150 students. By the time my grandfather arrived in 1903, there were beautiful new dormitories, a refectory, and an infirmary on campus. The growth was too much, too fast, and the school didn't work as designed. The experience at the school failed to meet either student or parent expectations. And fundamentally, there weren't enough jobs to accommodate the graduating apprentice farmers. In June 1903, Avigdor had a student revolt on his hands led by a large group of mostly Bulgarian students. The young men wrote both Avigdor and the Central Committee asking for farming placements in Bulgaria, or maybe Cyprus, or Argentina. They obviously wanted out of Djédéida. The Central Committee quickly replied that they would try to accommodate. Yet, by August 1903, Avigdor reports to the Central Committee that eleven, mostly Bulgarian, students were gone and that eight more might follow. Correspondence from Avigdor to the Committee gives a taste of the situation, as does a letter from former student Leon Israel to Avigdor. There's even a confiscated note from Israel to current students.

Writing to his recent classmates, Leon Israel is a firebrand revolutionary. Even though he's not at the school, he is still their "brother" and stands beside them. He holds up the example of revolutionary France and quotes Napoleon. "Impossible is not a French word." He tells them all is possible if they have the will. They must remain "stoic." He lays out how all the students in the school must petition the Alliance's Central Committee in Paris. They must write humbly, but firmly. All their meetings and correspondence must be held in the most secrecy. Israel even quotes and then paraphrases Karl Marx. Marx's "The emancipation of the workers must be the work of the workers themselves" becomes Israel's, "The emancipation of the students of the Farm School of Djédéida must be the work of the students themselves."

The efforts to keep Israel's letter secret from the school's administration obviously failed, since its copy is in the Alliance Archives in Paris.

Yet, in his January 3, 1904, letter to Director Avigdor, Israel did write humbly, but firmly. He first lays out the noble intentions of the school, its beautiful setting and exemplary facilities.

> The Farm School is situated in a pretty spot, it has a privileged location in all aspects; the Medjerda which cuts the vast domain in two, the train station, the post office, a verdant hill, a well, and a mill which give potable water. I daresay the scene is enchanting.
>
> Let us enter the school. We admire these beautiful gardens, even more so because they are the work of the students. The dwellings leave nothing to be desired. Two vast dormitories, an immense refectory, we are not squeezed at the Farm School!
>
> In crossing the well-tended fields, in visiting the beautiful installation of the Farm, in knowing the high and noble objective of the Alliance, in going through the educational and alimentary program of the students, in seeing the good health of these students, we say to ourselves: "Why, this is Eden, how these students must be happy!

Then, the complaints start. The program lies to the student about how much, and when, they must work in the fields. It's supposed to be a half-day in class and a half-day in the fields. Yet, sometimes they work days at a time in the field. The good jobs are always taken by the "advanced" students! Also, the food isn't up to snuff. The staff should sometimes eat with the students to monitor its quality. He calls the method of instruction "useless, arbitrary, [in short, it's] exploitation." The Director must remember, "The students are not laborers, they are before all else students!" Israel closes with the suggestion that with, "a bit more benevolence on your part, Monsieur le Directeur, Djédéida will truly be an Eden."

Avigdor isn't having it. Commenting on Israel's letter, the Director tells the committee that, "these students do not want to understand that in Djédéida we want to make agricultural workers and not office agronomists!" "The state of mind of our students can and must be attributed solely to the disproportion between their dreams, which the parents or those who sent them have inculcated in them, and the goal which we are seeking in Djédéida. The consequence is that the student revolts against this program and this timetable which does not respond to their fancies."

In letters over the next few years, Avigdor repeatedly asks that the Central Committee not send him any more students from Bulgaria, Turkey, or even Algeria. "The Bulgarian students are for the most part budding anarchists, quibblers, and rebels. They are stamped with despotism and not yet ready to intelligently practice liberty. The students want to judge their masters and condemn them. It's an impossible situation in which to run a school. They encourage their Turkish comrades. They are here to prepare for liberal careers, or commerce. They [only] want to learn French."

As a first-year "Turkish" student, my grandfather entered quite a situation. Quickly, Avigdor figured out how to right the ship. First, he cleaned house and expelled the troublemakers. He then made sure that the majority of students coming into the program were from North Africa. They were used to the weather, knew the language, and had local support from their families. Avigdor also reduced the total number of students to a size he thought he could reasonably teach, supervise, and place into work.

The materials taught at the school made a comprehensive course for practical agriculture, as well as a way to continue building well educated, modern Jews. After a 1905 visit, the vice president of the geographical society of Paris complimented the program. "I would like to say I had the satisfaction of finding in Tunisia a practical agricultural school that couldn't be better organized and put together."

The Course of Studies for my grandfather's second year at the school, 1904–1905, shows that first-year students continued subjects from their previous Alliance schools, including Hebrew, Jewish history, math, geometry, and French. The sciences of zoology, physics, chemistry, and botany were taught in the context of the students' future agricultural careers. Added to these classes were practical agriculture (the weeding, hoeing, and pruning so hated by Leon Israel), as well as the Arabic language.

Second- and third-year students continued their Hebrew, Jewish history, math, geography, and Arabic. Their science was organic chemistry. In agriculture class, they studied soils and animal husbandry, as well as agricultural technology, such as storing produce and harvesting and pressing grapes. They also learned practical geometry and basic architectural drawing. Additionally, since the farm school provided produce for Tunis, they learned all aspects of "truck farming."

Fourth- and fifth-year students really concentrated on the practical application of what they learned through "Agricultural Conferences." Naturally, they continued their French. Their math became focused on calculations necessary for farm work, as well as agricultural bookkeeping and record keeping. It was quite an education. We also know that a select group of students took English classes.

Victor apparently did well. The Alliance records have a May 22, 1904, report from Djédéida to Monastir and Mikevah Israel saying the "4 students give full satisfaction to their directors." On March 30, 1905, forty

Djédéida Farm School 1905. The arrow points to who I think might be Victor. (Courtesy of the Archives of the Alliance Israélite Universelle)

Left: Close up from 1905 Picture. Is this Victor? (Courtesy of the Archives of the Alliance Israélite Universelle) Right: Close up of Victor from 1920 photo. (Youcha family Photo)

francs arrived from Monastir for the town's students attending Djédéida: Haim Youcha, Elie Graciani, Samuel Cavo and Elie Massoth.

On July 2, 1905, we see that the principals in Mikevah and in Tunisia approved of the "Monastriote" students. Mr. Arié, the school director in Monastir, dreams his region will grow into a fertile field for agriculture, believing that the Jews are pioneers, especially those in agricultural schools. The effort continued. On August 14, 1905, two other students from Monastir, Samuel Farasez and Moise Israel, received admission to Djédéida.

The Alliance Archives also have incompletely labeled photos of the Farm School in Djédéida. Emre shared a photo of a group of farm school students, likely from 1905. One of the kids is labeled, Victor Chickly. We don't know the subject of the picture. Is it a class photo? Is it of the Bulgarian and Turkish students? To me, the latter is more likely because there's a wide range of ages in the photo. Regardless, there's a boy in the top left of the picture who could very well be my grandfather, Victor. He has a "Youcha face." He resembles pictures of my father, myself, and my son Zack at that age. He also looks very similar to the picture of Victor taken about 15 years later in New York. It's another thing we may never figure out, but I think it's him.

A fundamental problem for the school was they couldn't find work for students completing the program. The best solution was the Alliance buying land near the school and setting up a sharecropping system for its graduates. The method worked, but it was expensive and only served a small number of graduates. Attempts to set up similar sharecropping settings in the students' native communities didn't pan out. For example, there was a lot of correspondence about placing graduated students with an Ottoman landowner just outside of Monastir. Originally, Victor was to return home to Monastir as a trained farmer. It wasn't to be. There are no records of him ever having gone back home. We do know that those four additional students from Monastir went to Djédéida and that there was communication between Monastir and its sons at the farm school. It's also safe to assume there were letters home. Even though they depended on paper correspondence, which now seems inefficient, the Alliance was a tight community with communication between the different schools and Paris.

No one knew the problem of "job placement" better than the school's director, Samuel Avigdor, and he spoke truth to power. One year, the AIU President, Narcisse Leven, returned Avigdor's annual report. It was too pessimistic to be published in the Alliance's annual Bulletin. Avigdor didn't back down in his reply to his boss: "Did not one of our colleagues, with whom I keep up a fairly regular correspondence on the subject of the placement of our apprentices, go as far as to compare our agricultural mission to that statue of silver with feet of clay, and this because we desire for our students to install themselves outside of our sphere of action. As long as the work of agricultural education is not methodically

Farm School students at work. (Courtesy of the Archives of the Alliance Israélite Universelle)

systematically completed by the work of colonization, my colleague, in my opinion, will be correct; as soon as our students are removed from our benevolent [oversight], the parents, the town, and a thousand other circumstances lie in wait to turn them away from agricultural life."

Avigdor thought the place for the Alliance's students was with Jewish farming communities. In 1905, the Alliance spent 450 francs a year ($2,000 US dollars in 2022) to educate each student. Ideally, to make good on the investment, the Alliance sent the young men to appropriate Jewish farms elsewhere in the world.

Farm school graduates went to Argentina, Egypt, Cyprus, Bulgaria, and eventually even Canada. To solve the placement problem, the leaderships of the Alliance and its sister organization, the Jewish Colonization Association, were throwing stuff against the wall to see what stuck. The trouble was they weren't throwing clay against the wall, they were throwing young men's lives, including my grandfather's. And, it wasn't working so well, as my grandfather would soon experience. Following the path of one student, Jacob (Jacques, Jack) Mitrani illustrates how, and why, the Alliance ended up sending my grandfather to Canada.

Jacques Mitrani

Jacob, Jack, or Jacques, Mitrani's experiences illustrate the Alliance's problems with placing their graduates into jobs. Originally from Phillippopolis, today's Plovdiv in Bulgaria, Mitrani signed the June 8, 1903, Djedeida students' letter to Director Avigdor asking that students be able to do their 5th year of school in their home country. However, he doesn't appear to have been one of the revolt leaders.

The Mitrani name was well known within the Alliance. In the Alliance Archives, there are seven Mitranis listed as either teachers, school Deputy Directors, or Directors. Albert Mitrani served as the Deputy Director of the Alliance's school in Monastir. I have no idea if any of these Mitranis were related to Jacques. When Victor arrived at the farm school, Jacques Mitrani was already in his 4th year.

After attending the Alliance school in Phillippopolis, Mitrani was one of 38 students accepted to the farm school in 1900. Jacques and Victor met later in New York, where they lived and worked together on

W. 38th Street in Manhattan. By then, they obviously were friends. I'm not sure if they saw each other in between those times, but they traveled similar paths. Jacques Mitrani was the first student from the farm school at Djédéida to go to Canada. His method of traveling, his experiences, and his advice to the Alliance leadership, all helped determine my grandfather's experience.

Obviously lessening the number of potential Bulgarian troublemakers at his school and responding to the May 1904 student "revolt," Director Avigdor soon sent five fourth- and fifth-year Bulgarian students to work in Jewish farming colonies near Varna, Bulgaria, on the Black Sea. Jacques Mitrani went as one of three fourth-year students. By February 1905, it was clear that the placement hadn't worked out. A report from an investigator for the Alliance, M. Safarti, shows the boys were mistreated by the Russian Jewish colonists. The Russians, who were Ashkenazi, didn't like Sephardic Jews. When it got cold and there was no work in the fields, the Russian Jews refused to feed the Sephardic boy farmers. The boys had no choice but to leave the farms and go home. Avigdor says that if treated this way, any student would leave agriculture. Safarti suggests, and stresses, that if the Alliance really wanted to place these students in Bulgaria, the organization should directly buy land for them to farm.

The Alliance Archives again preserves correspondence discussing where the boys could go. Maybe Egypt? Maybe Canada? Maybe even Brazil? Avigdor asked if the JCA can arrange for Mitrani to go to Canada. In May 1905, Mitrani notified the Alliance that he was ready to go there and pursue his agricultural career. He got a letter of recommendation from the Paris office and headed to Montreal. Again, it didn't work out well.

From Jacques Mitrani's October 8, 1905, letter from Montreal to Avigdor, we know that even with a letter of recommendation, he wasn't able to see Mr. Ouriel, the president of the Baron de Hirsch Institute. Instead, he saw Ouriel's subordinate, Mr. Samuel, who ran what we now call "workforce development." Samuel advised Mitrani to not work with the Jewish colonists in Canada; they didn't pay well. Some advice from someone supposedly supporting the growth of Jewish farming colonies in Canada! While waiting for Samuel to help find him agricultural work,

Mitrani found his own with a Canadian market gardener near Montreal, but it only lasted a month.

With the idea of working in the Canadian West, Mitrani visited Samuel again at the JCA. Not only of no help, he was dismissive, saying, "Just because you have a letter from Paris, you think that we will give you everything you ask for!" According to Mitrani, Samuel told him if he wanted to go west, he should get a job with the railroad cleaning cars.

Avigdor and the Alliance supported Mitrani by writing another letter directly to the JCA in Montreal. Apparently, the letter never arrived, but in the resulting correspondence we get a real feeling of Avigdor's frustration about the placement of his graduates. "Who is this director of the Colonies that one always expects and who never comes!"

In March 1906, Avigdor implored Narcisse Leven, as President of both the Alliance and Jewish Colonization Association, to help find work for Mitrani by writing directly to the proper administrators in Montreal.

Avigdor also wrote about an article he read in an agricultural magazine regarding the Canadian government's incentives to potential farmers in the West. If no place can be found for Mitrani in the Jewish colonies in Canada, Avigdor declared that they would find a place for him themselves.

In the meantime, Mitrani visited the Montreal JCA offices every week for three months. It's painful reading the letters describing the bureaucratic brush off he continually got from the JCA officials, but his experience illustrates the lack of coordination between the Alliance and its sister organization, the JCA. Even though led by the same people, the staffs weren't coordinated, and it was the young people put in their care who suffered.

From reading the AIU correspondence, we learn a lot about the Djédéida school director, Samuel Avigdor. Obviously not always easy to get along with, he was also intelligent, passionate, and dogged, clearly committed to the purpose of the school, as well as his students. When his wife died in 1904, he hardly pauses in his work. He didn't give up on the idea of sending his students to Canada.

Avigdor had one person in Canada he trusted. He wrote Mitrani asking for his thoughts about settling farm school students in western

Canada. On April 13, 1906, Mitrani replied with his observations and advice.

- "The West of Canada is the most favorable land for us, the students of the Farm school who have a good knowledge of agriculture, and who can quickly pass the other colonists who have never touched the work."
- From the stories he hears, the area is "stable" and it's "straightforward" getting there.
- The best time for finding work is in the end of July.
- The Alliance will need a good agent in Winnipeg to select the best farms and land near villages or towns.
- In order for the work placements to not end badly, the correct placement is "vitally important."
- If the students decide to come to Canada, they must be "committed to agriculture." If they're just coming to see the country or work in commerce, it's better that they don't come at all. They will be quickly disillusioned.
- Unless they are working in Montréal or Québec, English is absolutely necessary. "The man who doesn't know the language suffers immensely when trying to find a job."
- Picking the right students is imperative. He thinks that four is the correct number. They must have a lot of "goodwill and energy to overcome all the obstacles in their way. They'll need the qualities of sobriety and initiative that were imparted at the school."
- The Alliance must also give students some financial support that will take care of, and protect them, a little bit.
- He also suggests the Alliance should help its successful students eventually buy land. He thinks it will cost about $2,000 to do this, and the loan would be paid back in 3 to 4 years. This suggestion mimics programs of the Canadian government and the Canadian Pacific Railroad.

Even though Mitrani was only about 21 and had never been west of Montreal, he gave good advice. Avigdor and the Alliance took most of it. It's the suggestions they didn't follow that caused problems for my grandfather and his fellow students.

Victor Goes to Canada

"...we must continue our attempt to transform these young people from the city into farmers, to strengthen their constitutions and to develop in them the qualities of energy, endurance, and sobriety which make the true peasant."

—Narcisse Leven From *50 Years* (1912)

Leven's objective wasn't going to be easy. Jacques Mitrani's experience with the Russian Jewish farmers in Bulgaria wasn't unique. Avigdor reported on the experience of farm school graduates in Algeria.

> Badly treated, dismissed as soon as their Jewish origin was known, the impression produced in the public by the odyssey of these unfortunate people young people was profound; one saw in them the living proofs of the impossibility for the Jews to live by the farming profession.

With the hope that Canada would be a better place for his graduates, Avigdor got the OK from the Central Committee in late 1906 to prepare his students for the placement. He assembled likely and willing students, and M. Cohen, an instructor at the Farm School, started teaching them English. By February 6, 1907, Avigdor chose a group of four to go, pending their parents' approval. My grandfather, Victor Youchah was not one of them. Within a week, Avigdor wrote M. Leven,

> February 11, 1907
> Mr. President,
>
> Following your letter of February 6th, I must inform you that the young Guido Enriquez will not be going to Canada, his parents were opposed. We are replacing him with the young

Youchah, in 4th year, from Monastir, aged 18, who has just made me aware of his desire to settle himself in Canada.

Having "just" made the Director aware of his interest, Victor's decision likely was on the spur of the moment. We don't know for sure, but can assume, that he was in M. Cohen's English class, otherwise he shouldn't have been eligible to go. Victor was a fourth-year student with 3½ years of agricultural schooling. Everybody else selected to go were fifth-years with 4½ years' experience. Maybe the original plan was for him to go the following year? Regardless, he stepped into the open slot.

On February 24th Mitrani wrote Nissim Hazan, one of the students planning to go to Canada, with advice that echoes his letter to Avigdor. Learn English. Only come if you're going to do agricultural work. Mitrani also said to not visit your parents before departing. It would only cost money and cause pain. Victor apparently took this advice a step further and didn't even tell his parents before he committed to going.

On the 13th of March 1907, Benjamin Boccara, Nissim Hazan, Albert Foua, and Haim Youcha embarked on a ship of the Florio & Rubatino Company in Tunis headed to Genoa. They departed Genoa on April 4th, arrived in New York on April 21st, and must have continued to Montreal to meet their friend, "Ancell, President du Baron de Hirsch Fund." After that, they made it to Winnipeg.

In 1907, Winnipeg was developing from a frontier town into a farming, mercantile, and railroad center. With 8,000 Jews, it had the third largest Jewish population in Canada behind Montreal (40,000) and Toronto (10,000). The city was a three-day train ride from Montreal. Letters from the JCA in Montreal to Paris make clear that the Montreal office would not be able to closely supervise the youths, but they would try their best.

We know from Alliance correspondence and reports in the annual Bulletin that in the Spring of 1907 the Alliance sent two groups of farm school candidates to Canada. One group came from Djédéida, the other consisted of, in part, past students from the Mikevah Israel farm school in Palestine. The rest were just enthusiastic Alliance students from other schools, with no agricultural training, mostly from Bulgaria and

Constantinople. How exactly my grandfather's group got to out to Winnipeg is unknown. We do know that their communication skills were not strong. Within a month a worried Joseph Foua wrote the Alliance for news about his brother, Albert.

A letter from an Alliance student who hadn't gone to either farm school gives a sense of the idealism and enthusiasm the young men felt for the tasks and opportunities in Canada. On March 17, 1907, N. Menassé writes from Viden, a town near Winnipeg, to his Alliance school director, M. Fresco in Constantinople.

Dear Sir,

> I am writing to you with the purpose of giving more ample details about Canada. I wish to inform you that I currently find myself in the Canadian west. At the time of my previous letter to you, I was not fully informed of everything. The 10th of this month in the company of my 3 companions we left Montreal for Winnipeg, the central city of the Canadian West. In that city there is an institute for the emigrants of all countries. We were lodged there for 15 days free of charge. During this interval special agents of the government were charged with securing places [for us].
>
> The day after our arrival in Winnipeg we left for Virden in the company of a government agent, from where I write to you now. The news had already spread in the commune that 4 professional farmers were seeking work. You should've seen how they rushed to surround us! Last year, in the province of Manitoba alone, there was a shortage of 20,000 workers; this year fearing the same penury of labor it was to whoever would hire us. What would you say if I told you that I was engaged to work for 125 francs a month and that I have in addition to that room, board, laundry etc., I who in fact know nothing of agriculture? Whereas my companions will make 130 francs. In August, September, and October we make double. In winter no work on the farms. But, we can still otherwise make 125/130 francs per month, there

being no shortage of work. By this fact we are sure that towards the end of the year we will have saved 1,500 to 1,800 francs; that's all that is needed for a person to establish himself. Land costs nothing; tools and all that is necessary for agriculture are advanced with annual payments. The first year one just makes ends meet; the second one frees oneself of all debts; the third one lives like a prince on his land.

This was the dream. A "Promised Land" for Jewish farmers. It was the dream of the Alliance, and the dream of their farm school students. It was a dream soon crushed.

A letter from the Paris office of the JCA to the Paris office of the Alliance exudes institutional arrogance. "We have punctually recommended to the Committee in Montreal the four young people from Djédéida who have emigrated to Canada. We suppose that this committee will have taken care of their placement." Their supposition was painfully wrong.

A letter found in the JCA Archives in Montreal makes it clear that the Alliance and JCA botched their job placement responsibility by delegating it to "government agents." Correct placement was the aspect of the program Mitrani said was most important for success, and the supervising adults blew it. On July 18, 1907, the agent in Winnipeg writes to M. Samuel at the Baron de Hirsch Institute,

Dear Sir,

In compliance with your instructions of July 8 I beg to say the following are the boys I have located namely Hazan, Yusha, David Levin, Nissim Eli. These four boys are in Winnipeg and working as follows, Hazan and Yusha are working in Rogers Fruit Wholesale but their job will not last very long. The reason they did not stay on the farm was because they thought the work was too hard for them… My opinion on the four boys I met is that they won't make farmers in this country. The first reason after asking them different questions is that they claim the work is too hard. Second, the farming in this country is so different to the farming they are used to but I don't think they will ever get adopted to it.

My idea is that if the ICA [JCA] wants to learn young people to become farmers in Canada they should establish an agricultural school in Canada and teach them the Canadian ways and methods—not to have them trained in [Jaffa] or other places where the farming is entirely different and when they come to this country first they cannot talk the language and second they've got to start the work over again which is harder than if they had never done any agricultural work.

This wasn't the first time the Alliance heard this message about placing students abroad. The agricultural practices and work habits taught in Djédéida didn't transfer well to other locations.

And what happened to the enthusiastic young M. Menassé? In his letter, the agent reported the young man was on his way back to Montreal. By December 1907, Benjamin Bochara was back home in Tunis. Albert Foua's parents evidentially moved to Montreal where he joined them. Nissim Hazzan stayed and persevered. What he went through sounds awful. Avigdor sent Paris an extract of a letter dated "February 12, 1908, from the student Hazan established in Canada":

> I inform you that 4 months ago [October 1907] I left the city to come and work in the countryside on a farm located 60 miles from Winnipeg near Lake Manitoba. In winter there is a great lack of work in town; especially this year which was one of the worst, in relation to harvests. In Winnipeg several factories have stopped working this winter, because they have no work to occupy their employees. The result is that thousands of people hang out in the streets and eat all their savings. Others go to the countryside to work just for their food. Lumber contractors do not hire many men, because it is difficult to get the sawn timber out. The wood is hauled in sled carts, but as there is not enough snow the sleds cannot be used. This is still one of the causes of

the misery that reigns in Winnipeg, as well as in most cities in Canada.

I signed up for the whole winter with a French-Canadian farmer with not very high wages. I consider myself happier than others who only work for their food.

I am responsible for taking care of 30 heads of animals (oxen, cows, calves). From time to time I carry a few loads of hay, the stacks of which are 2 or 3 miles from the farm. In addition, I am in charge of carting and cutting wood for the heating of the apartments and other small jobs. Moreover, in these times there are only these works to be done in the country, at least in Manitoba where the cold is very rigorous. The region where I am is a livestock region, there is almost no cultivation. In summer some vegetables are grown for household consumption. And in the months of July-August we take care of making hay to winter the animals. During the seven or eight months of the year the animals do not return to the barn, they find enough food in the fields. But in winter, as the pastures are completely lacking, the farmer is obliged to provide them with food throughout the bad season. On the farm I am well fed and well housed. Only one obstacle prevents me from staying in the countryside for a long time: it is the anti-Semitism of the French Canadians. I assure you, Mr. Director, that it is the most difficult thing to pass off as French and Catholic, especially in matters of religion. We find ourselves quite often embarrassed and we have difficulty getting out of trouble. I have been here for 4 months and my mother and my parents have not heard from me nor have I heard from them. The gate office being five miles from the house I cannot carry the letter myself. And since they are used to reading addresses, it is impossible for me to correspond with my parents.

Every Sunday we have to go to Mass and do a lot of ceremonies that I've never seen. All of this contributes to unwittingly alienating me from our true religion. You can well imagine, Director, that it is impossible to lead such a life. I can't wait for spring to arrive so I can go back to town where, at least, we don't have to fight with fanatics all the time.

Benjamin Boccara, then in Tunis, added to Avigdor's report his comments about his experience in Canada.

> In Canada we only work in agriculture for 4 months in the summer. Livestock are also kept in summer. While in winter all the work consists of clearing snow from the streets, cutting wood, and transporting it in sleds, or finally engaging in trade for a low wage. One can never work a whole year in the same house, or on the same farm; except among the rich farmers where one always has to take care of the cattle. Unfortunately, the fanaticism and the anti-Semitism of the Canadian farmers, mean that the Jewish workers are obliged to become very good Catholics, and to go with their bosses every Sunday to mass. The Jews and even the Protestants are never received on the farms.

Boccara was called "The Protestant" because he refused to pray. Avigdor adds his own thoughts to the Committee on March 8th,

> Mr. President,
>
> The attached extracts from the correspondence that I have just received from our former students sent to Canada will edify you on their unenviable situation and on the difficulties caused by their placement in French farms. The last letter from the young Hazan is particularly instructive; under pain of being recognized as a Jew or a Protestant, he can correspond only with his parents; he is obliged to go to church and participate in religious ceremonies; this report has been confirmed by a second student Boccara who is currently in Djédéida and who would return to Canada only to work in town, in Montreal. All these young people rushed to this country, lacking material support and without hope of establishing themselves in homesteads, will inevitably return to

commercial occupations in town; it seems that in Canada, among cultivators, [there is] as much anti-Semitism as in the colonies of Algeria and Tunisia.

Please accept, Mr. President, the assurance of my devoted sentiments.

S. Avigdor

Since the Winnipeg agent reported in July that Boccara was already back in Montreal, and obviously on his way to Tunis, we can assume that his experience was similar to my grandfather's, the one that drove him from the dream of the farm to work for the Rogers Fruit Wholesale company at 85 Lombard St., Winnipeg, Canada.

The investigation by the Jewish agencies continued. Too bad the Alliance administration and JCA didn't put as much effort into planning the project as they did compiling an "after action report" about its failure.

On March 6, 1908, the JCA's investigation in Winnipeg reported about work conditions at the farms.

Sirs,

We have occupied ourselves, on various occasions, with the matter of the placement in Canada of the young people from our agricultural schools. We believe it will be useful to transmit to you a communication which we received today from our agent in Winnipeg. After having spoken about the students from our farm school of Slobodka-Lesna, our correspondent adds:

With reference to the boys sent from the Orient during 1907, I regret to say that our experiences shows [sic] that the experiment of sending out those boys to Canada has proven an absolute failure, for the following reasons.

The work here is by far harder than that in the Orient.

The climate is absolutely different from what they are used to. The consequences therefore was this [sic], that almost all of these boys had to leave for the South and California, where the work is easier and the climate more suitable. Therefore, I would strongly advise not to send any more of that class of school graduates to Canada."

Please receive, Sirs, the assurance of our distinguished sentiments.

The Alliance certainly did a lousy job preparing the way for their students, but was it really the kids' fault?

The Alliance's farm students were meant to be the implementers of a dream, the dream of Jews going back to the land. The Alliance's objective was to raise up the downtrodden and make them leaders in this noble movement. Pretty paternalistic, but still a noble attitude. Jacques Mitrani's letter makes clear the students' devotion to agriculture, as well as their knowledge about how much the Alliance invested in their education. A lack of training doesn't make an 18-year-old give up on a dream for which they've spent more than a quarter of their life preparing. Running into raw hatred, possibly for the first time, certainly can. Nissim Hazan's correspondence with Samuel Avigdor illustrates the role of anti-Semitism in the failure of the Alliance students as farmers.

On November 15, 1909, Avigdor wrote the Central Committee telling about a letter from Hazan who spent almost three years living in western Canada under deplorable conditions. Yes, the winters were harsh, but it was the anti-Semitism of the Canadian farmers that he couldn't stand. Hazzan hid his religion and used a fake name. In Hazan's October 26, 1909, letter from Minnewakan (Manitoba), he wanted to return to work in Djédéida, in his eyes "the sole refuge for us unhappy students." From there, Avigdor wanted to send him elsewhere in Europe or Africa. What's going on was clear to Avigdor. "Nizzim Hazan is not suffering because of unemployment, but because he is a Jew." The AIU then authorized Avigdor to hire Hazan to work at Djédéida for three or four months.

Isolated on a farm, in a hostile environment, there's almost no choice but to flee for safety. In the cases of the young men from the farm school, safety was initially the city of Winnipeg with its Jewish population, then Montreal, or home, or the farm school, even America. In all of the Alliance's correspondence after July 1907, there's no word about my grandfather. His friends don't know where he is, neither does his family. He doesn't seem to have fled to any of the same places as the other students. Victor is "lost" in Western Canada.

Jacob Searches for His Lost Victor

Preserved in the Alliance Archives are letters from my great grandfather, Jacob Isaac Youchah. Of all the research work, the discovery of these letters most profoundly impacted my family. Jacob wrote both to Samuel Avigdor, the Director of the farm school in Djédéida and Narcisse Leven, the President of the Alliance in Paris. Jacob didn't care that these are powerful people. He was looking for his son.

Occurring over a period of 14 months, the letters tell the story of a father becoming more distraught as time passed. These letters correct mistakes and clear up inconsistencies in my family's stories. They give us an example of Jacob's signature which confirms the spelling of our name in Hebrew. They also confirm that he was a *Mouktar* and give us the Ottoman name of the neighborhood he administered, Ali Tchaouch. The letters create new questions and offer new understanding to family behavior. More than that, they give us a little bit of what Jacob must have been like. The letters, with the existing bureaucratic responses, speak for themselves.

Monastir the 6th of September 1908

To Mr. Narcisse Leven President of the Alliance Israelite Universelle Paris
Mr. President

My son, Haim Youchah, student of the Djédéida Farm-School, after having completed his five years of study, was sent by the Alliance to Canada with some other classmates of his. Since that time, I have suffered the misfortune of receiving absolutely no news of my only son. That is why I have to come to beg you, in your goodness, to please write to the establishments in Canada in order to obtain information about my son, seeing as the aforementioned was sent there by you alone. I am persuaded that your investigations will bear fruit.

In the hope that you will kindly return some measure of calm to a poor old father who lives only for his son, please accept, Mr. President, my respectful sentiments, of a profound gratitude, with which, I have the honor of being your very humble servant,

Jacob Youchah

Monastir the 10th of November 1908
Mr. President, Paris.

I have the pain of exposing to you the suffering that I am experiencing due to the lack of news of my only son. Some time ago I wrote to you about this matter, I have received no response. I do not wish that you should return my son to me, although the aforementioned left by your order; I only wish to know where he is and to have news of him. I beg you, to please take the necessary steps, of which the Alliance alone is capable, and to thus calm the anxieties of a father who would lose his mind over [his son]. The student in question, attended the Farm-School in Djédéida for 4 years, and is called Haim Youchah.

In the hope that you will send me, the happy result of your steps, please accept, Mr. President, the eternal gratitude of your very humble servant,

Jacob Youchah

November 12, 1908, letter from Samuel Avigdor to Paris:

Here is a copy of a letter which addresses the case of an old student of Djédéida. Do you have any news about the young man?

November 16, 1908 letter from Samuel Avigdor to Central Committee:

> Former student Haim Youchah: We ask the J.C.A. to please have one of your agents in Canada make inquiries to pick up the trail of this young man.

November 22, 1908, letter from Alliance to JCA, Paris:

> The father of one of our former students in Djédéida, Haim Youchah, who left for Canada in April 1907 with 3 of his classmates, is asking us what has happened to his son, about whom he has had no news for months and months. We would be very obliged if you would kindly instruct one of your Canadian agents to make inquiries to find the [illegible] and the current residence of this young man.

November 24, 1908, letter from JCA, Paris, to Alliance:

> We have written to our friends in Montreal, as you asked us in your letter dated the 22nd of this month, to beg them to inform us of the lot of the the young Haim Jouchah [sic]. We will not hesitate to communicate with you their response and beg you to accept, Sirs, the assurance of our distinguished sentiments.

> [two signatures]

November 27, 1908, postcard from Alliance to Jacob Youchah:

> Sir,

> In response to your letter of November 10th, we have the honor of informing you that the Jewish Colonization Association

will conduct, through its agents in Canada, inquiries into what has happened to your son. As soon as we have been made known the result of their inquiries, we will communicate them to you.

Please accept, sir, the assurance of our best wishes.

Secretary,

December 17, 1909, letter from Jacob Youcha to the President of the AIU:

Monastir the 17th of December 1909

To M. Narcisse Leven, President of the Alliance Israelite Universelle in Paris

Mr. President,

On the 27th of November 1908 you sent me a letter/card informing me that the Jewish Colonization Association would have its Canadian agents investigate/search on what has become of my son. 13 months have gone by without me receiving any detail, any clue, about him.

The Alliance, when leaving Monastir for Djédèida at the time of Mr. Arié [The Alliance Monastir Boys' School Director in 1903], had asked for my consent. Why didn't we do it when he was sent to Canada? You can see that all of this is an absolute negligence from your directors who hardly care about them only/except to have them expatriated. This is how they hide the flaws of their small capability. They needed to be more conscientious.

This is a panicked/distraught father that is talking, forgive my fair criticisms. I want my only son to be returned to me! The Alliance has [the] means, it should use them. I am done for, my whole family is done for!!...

Where are the J.C.A. investigations/searches?

Is this how your directors deal with the delicate questions entrusted to them. Because we are far from our sons (son), we can't defend our sons' (son's) interests. That the Tunisian fathers must be happy? They are close to them and closely defend their interests. These abuses of confidence have rendered my life very bitter. The/His mother doesn't exist anymore, she died of grief/pain, do you want to end my days through a suicide???

In the hope that you would want to seriously take care of my son's search, and make a brother happy, accept, Mr. President, with all the affliction/sorrow that my situation entails, the assurance of my gratitude for everything that you would have done for me.

The unfortunate father
Jacob Youchah

P.S. Please take note that my son is named Victor (Haim) Jacob Youchah

December 17, 1909, letter from Jacob Youcha to Samuel Avigdor. The same day as he wrote Narcisse Leven:

To Mister Avigdor, Director of the Farm-School, in Djédéida, Tunisia

Mr Directeur—On the 14th of April 1908, you promised me to look into the whereabouts of my son. You ended your letter by saying "I will write to you just as soon as I have the answer". Now that it's been 20 months, should I still be expecting to hear from you? Is this how you care for the children whose care is entrusted to you? The mother suffered to death. Do you want to kill me as well? Look into this matter, look seriously into this matter, for you have all the means at your disposal. I want my son. Didn't this painful delay of 20 months give you any result?

December 17, 1909. Letter from Jacob to Narcisse Leven. (Courtesy of the Archives of the Alliance Israélite Universelle)

Jacob Isaac Ishach's signature in Soletreo. Possibly his post script in French.

In the hopes that you will want to comfort a father (and the mother who is no more), please continue looking into this further.

December 31, 1909, letter from Samuel Avigdor to the President of the AIU:

Mr. President,

Former student Youcha:

Nearly three years ago, this young man left for Canada, and we haven't heard anything from him since; I'd written to you about him before to strongly request/beg on behalf of the parents that you look into the matter on my end, I had written and received no answer. The father just sent me a letter which I've attached. I had Mr. Benveniste reply to the father, and let him know that I'm only responsible for the children in Djédéida. I'm begging you once again to verify that there are in fact no means available to track this boy by contacting Jewish societies and colonies in Canada.

Changes in Family Stories

My grandfather Victor arrived in New York in 1910, walked into a Sephardic coffee shop on the Lower East Side, and met a fellow Monastirli. Finding out that Victor is Jacob's son, this man told Victor that soon after he left for Tunisia his mother died. His father then remarried and had a second family. All this happened with Jacob never telling Victor a word. What kind of father doesn't tell his son that his mother died? And keeps that secret for seven years? Jacob doing so, and Victor's resulting anger, caused an understandable rupture between father and son.

That's a foundational family story. It's made Jacob out to be a bad guy, an anomaly in this family. The family stories don't line up with the information in the letters from the Alliance Archives. Jacob's letters changed my father's perception of his grandfather, and, at 94, gave him more insight into his own father.

In the stories passed down to me from my dad, Jacob was a real son of a bitch. That other "not nice" family story telling how Jacob slapped Victor so hard on the face that he left finger marks just reinforced the impression of Jacob as an S.O.B. into a "black and white" image.

The Alliance letters change this perception. Jacob writes that his wife, Anna, died of "grief" after Victor was lost, probably in early-, or mid-, 1909. Not in 1903 or 1904 soon after Victor left for school in Tunisia. And, although Jacob did remarry, it wasn't until after 1910, after he likely knew his son was safe in New York. We'll never know Anna's official cause of death, but we know that her husband blamed it on their only son having gone missing.

The letters also make brutally clear Jacob's love for his son. He's not asking for the return of his son, only for the knowledge that he is alive and safe. Jacob writes Narcisse Leven as a father appealing to another father. In the powerful December 17th letter, Jacob criticizes the Alliance's handling of Victor's situation. His tone and attitude indicate someone used to managing people. This fits with his being a *Mouktar* and having an official position in the Ottoman hierarchy. The employees of the Alliance obviously botched the job, only incompetence or stupidity can explain this. Now, as the man in charge, it is Leven's responsibility to fix the mess. Otherwise, a father's grief will make Jacob kill himself. This last claim might seem a little melodramatic, but he makes his point. Jacob has lost his son and his wife. He's responsible for taking care of a young daughter. Living was not good. Yet, these are not the letters of a cowering supplicant. As a result of his position in France, his leadership in both the Alliance and the Jewish Colonization Association, Narcisse Leven is one of the most powerful European Jews in the eyes of the Sephardim. Jacob writes him strongly and directly.

The Story's Effect on My Dad, and Myself

After I received a copy of the December 17 letter from Emre, I did a rough translation of the letter and called my dad. I was worried that he wouldn't receive it well. It disassembled several of the family assumptions he'd held for over 90 years. I was afraid he might block it out, as he has some previous information, but that wall was truly gone.

When we talked about the letters, it was a moving conversation. The information really changed my dad's perception of his grandfather, which is something I was trying to do. Or, at least I hoped to find information to make that possible. The "link in the chain" theory says that qualities are passed down from one generation to the next. Jacob didn't fit. Dad's father, my grandfather Victor, was a quietly strong, loving man. With such a negative view of Jacob, my dad always thought that his father must have gotten these qualities only from his mother, Anna, and that she must have been an incredible, loving woman. Anna certainly may have had those qualities, but I felt this view was also too "black and white."

When my dad and I spoke about the letters, he said he always "couldn't figure this man out. Now it completes the fabric." "It makes it fit." Jacob was like a "fracture in the line of who we are." My dad "couldn't understand this man." Now, he said this information about his grandfather "puts me in peace. It's a gift." As a son, I couldn't ask for anything more.

A rupture between a father and child is a terrible thing. It leaves its effect for generations. I've felt the results of Jacob and Victor's falling out my whole life, and not just through my father's stories. My father distanced himself from his father. I did the same. At the start of this family research, I worried I was watching the same thing happen between myself and my kids. Was it because strong parental personalities force children to create their own space? Or, is this a family legacy of Jacob and Victor's rupture?

Probably both, and more. One thing I know is that by doing this research, I gained a more rounded view of Jacob, as has my dad. My relationship with my dad also got better. Making regular monthly Pandemic visits to his house combined with oud lessons with Ara, didn't hurt (I told Ara several times that he'd made me a better son.) A lot of the bettering relationship came from discussions about his relationship with his father, and Victor's relationship with Jacob. We also, indirectly, talked about our relationship.

Why is the Family Story About Jacob Wrong?

According to my father and his sister, Aunt Beck, my grandfather never talked much about his life before coming to New York. My dad certainly never spoke to him about it. Whatever stories my father learned were because he had "big ears" and overheard other people's conversations. Or he heard the stories from his mother.

I loved my grandmother, my Grandma Frieda. She was one of the strongest people I've ever known. Her life story is another book. She gave joy and love. She also was very tough. Orphaned and working since she was eight, she took Social Security at age 65 and finally lived her childhood. I remember all the paintings, sculptures, and basketball trophies in her ocean view Coney Island apartment. (I also remember sticking to the vinyl couch covers during humid summer visits.) My grandmother was extremely independent and opinionated. She was also incredibly loyal to her husband. Through decades of widowhood, my father always said she never looked at another man. I've watched my father repeat this behavior after the death of my mom. During the research we learned from Grandma's favorite granddaughter (my cousin Linda Fier) that after World War Two ended and probably when my dad was going to college in Florida, Frieda went to California to look up a past beau. She came back realizing she made the right choice in marrying Victor. (The discovery of this story hasn't changed my dad's views or actions.)

Frieda's loyalty to her husband may have made her switch up stories about Victor a little bit. For instance, my grandmother was the source of the story of my grandfather possibly going to Palestine. Uncle Morris disagreed. Now, I know why. As a Monastirli and first cousin, Uncle Morris knew the story of Victor being "lost in Canada." The rupture between Victor and Jacob happened. That couldn't be denied. In my grandmother's story, the fault was Jacob's, the father-in-law she would never meet.

It's likely that Jacob did cause the rupture, just as it's likely that he slapped his son's face. Jacob's letters make clear that he was a powerful, passionate person. This makes sense in my father's family. Once Victor turned up in New York, Jacob very well may have blamed him for Anna's death and said he didn't want to talk to him anymore. I can't know this, but something inside of me feels it to be, if not "the truth," at least a strong possibility.

What This Must Have Meant to Victor

Last seen on the prairies of Western Canada, he appears in a coffee shop in New York. It's easy to imagine the feelings of the Monastirli who "found him." The story of his being lost would have been a big deal. Victor's father was the neighborhood "mayor." His mother died of grief at Victor's disappearance. Even though Jacob signed the letters to Narcisse Leven, he signed them in the Ladino script, Solitreo. Someone else fluent in French obviously wrote the letters. The Jewish community wasn't that large. Word was out on the street. Victor, one of the community's few students to receive an Alliance scholarship, was lost. Scholarship students were a big deal. The community obviously followed the students' progress. The son of the Alliance's school Director in Monastir even visited the farm school in Djédéida. Although it appears that Victor never went back home for a visit, the Monastirlis he left behind followed his progress. There must have been expectations. He had disappeared. Now, he was found.

The communities in New York and Monastir were closely linked, and the big wave of emigration was just starting. A "little" Monastir centered around Chrystie and Allen Streets in New York City, the likely location of the coffee shop. Victor's story almost certainly was told in the community. The fate of the young men sent from Monastir to the agricultural school in Tunisia was still mentioned almost 20 years later in reports about the history of education in the Bitolan Jewish Community. When Victor walked into that Lower East Side coffee shop in 1910, his story must have been well known in both Monastir and New York.

After reading many hundreds of pages about the school where he was educated and the culture it tried to instill, I get the feeling he may have felt more like a French-speaking citizen of the world, than a traditional Sephardic Jew from the Balkans. When Victor got the opportunity to go to Canada, as with most 18-year-olds, he looked forward, not back. He didn't ask his parents' permission to go to Canada; he went.

He was only 21 at the time of the coffee shop encounter. He was living his own life's adventure, and it hadn't been easy. To hear that his mother died, that his father was looking for him, and that his story was known to the whole community, must have been very hard. It's easy to see how he could blame himself, at least in part, for his mother's death, a terrible thing with which to live.

From all the family stories, Victor was a loving, quiet man. He never struck his children to discipline them. He instilled the love that was still evident on my 94-year-old Aunt Beck's face the last time I saw her speak about him—almost 75 years after he died. For me, it's easy to see why he wouldn't talk about his life before coming to New York. He'd have to explain too much and relive the pain.

My dad always felt distanced from his father. There were no deep conversations between them. They never talked about his father's past. When my dad asked his mother about this, she said Victor was waiting for his sons to become men before he really talked to them. That time never came. Victor died when my dad was seventeen. I'm certainly grateful to have been able to talk with my dad, even though some of the conversations we had when I was a teenager caused the distance between us. The recent conversations about the family history have patched a lot of that up.

My dad asked me throughout my research, "Why was I doing it?" "What did I hope to find?" "What was I getting out of it?" Part of my response was always that I hoped to learn more about relationships between parents and children in our family. I hoped that it would help me better understand my relationship with him, as well as my relationships with my own kids.

Finding the letters from Jacob, and being able to make a more sensible picture of him, certainly took me a long way down that path.

New York 1910

Victor Gets to NY

How Victor got to New York in 1910 is another well-known family story, and, as far as we can tell, this one turned out to be true.

Elias Alazraki wanted to raise his daughter. A young Sephardic man working in Montreal as a laborer in a foundry, he married Elizabeth Tapp, a local Catholic woman. Their daughter, Esther, was born in Montreal October 28, 1908. Within a year, Elizabeth died, and Esther likely was returned to the care of her grandmother, Ellen Tapp. All this Jessica, my wife the archivist, figured out from Montreal church records and US immigration documents during an evening of online research.

Elias's best friend was Victor Youcha. The two men kidnapped Esther and came to New York. We don't know about the "kidnapping" aspect of the story, but we do know that Elias, Victor, and Esther all were on the same train when they emigrated from Montreal to New York in January 1910. Another family story involving my grandmother, when researched, confirms the connection.

In 1912, during the Balkan War, a major battle occurred in Kir Kilisse, Turkey, the home of my grandmother Fortune, Victor's future wife. At fourteen, Fortune was already an orphan. The battle separated her from her siblings for several months and she was forced to sew soldiers' uniforms to survive. These soldiers were mostly Sephardic Jews in the Bulgarian Army with whom she could speak Ladino. They paid her in gold. She started working for her family when she was eight. Yet, this was the first time she ever got paid. She sewed those coins into her coat, and when reunited with her family, told no one.

Jewish Bulgarian soldiers after battle of Kir Kilisse. (Zack Youcha photo from Kirklareli synagogue)

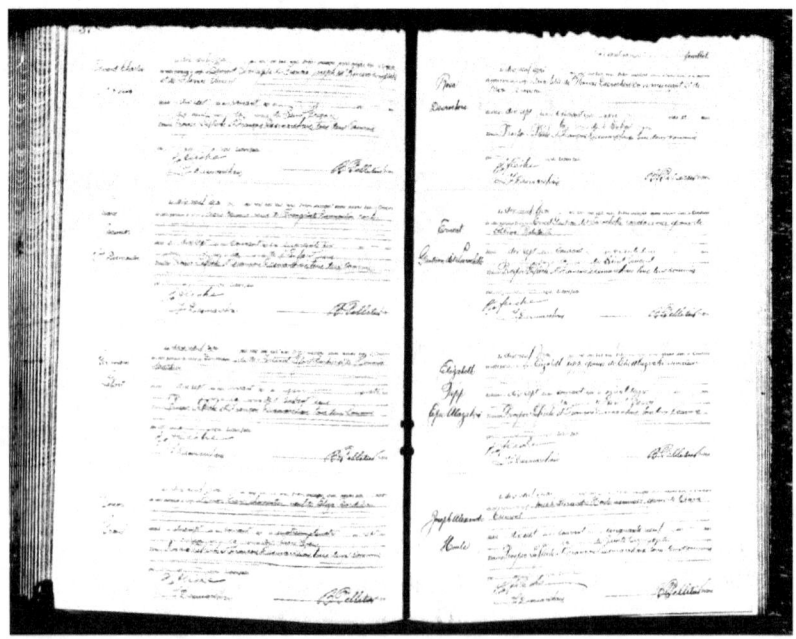

Montreal Church record of Esther Alazracki's birth. (Retrieved from Ancestry.com)

What Kind of Past 111

Record of Victor, Elias, and Esther Alazraki entering the United States. (Retrieved from Ancestry.com)

Arriving at Ellis Island in 1913 with her brother, Robert (Bohor), the immigration officials nearly sent them back. Their brother Lazar failed to meet them, and if they couldn't produce enough money to show they could survive, they would return to the port from which they sailed. Fortune had the money in her coat. She said nothing. She knew her brothers would take it for themselves.

Lazar eventually showed up, and two years later young Fortune married Victor Youcha. Naturally, she told her new husband about the gold coins. He soon lent them to his good friend Elias Alazraki to start a successful produce business. Elias never paid Victor back, and Victor didn't want to embarrass his friend by asking. In the meantime, Fortune stewed; she was not a person you wanted to make angry.

When Victor died in 1945, at only 56, my grandmother went up to the Alazrachi's apartment on the Grand Concourse in the Bronx to collect. They paid her back the principal, but no interest on the 30-year loan. Fortune stayed angry.

Working on 38th Street. Living with Jacques Mitrani

Victor arrived in New York in early March 1910. By June 1st, the 1910 US Census tells us he was living with his old, influential farm school friend Jacques Mitrani on W. 38th Street. From the information in the Census, it seems that they lived above a restaurant where they both worked.

Making his way from the Canadian prairie to Victoria, British Columbia, Mitrani arrived in San Francisco by the end of October in 1907. Probably one of the farm school students reported by the Canadian government agent as going to California to pick oranges, Jacques' time in California didn't last long. By early 1910, he traveled from California to Detroit, entering Canada at Windsor, Ontario. In late February, just a few weeks before Victor, Jacques Mitrani arrived in New York via Montreal. (One hundred and twelve years later, the Youcha and Mitrani families reconnected as a result of Emre's research and Facebook.)

By the 1915 census, Victor and Fortune, his wife of 2 months, lived at 135 Orchard Street, in the middle of the Sephardic community on the Lower East Side. The Sephardim kept to themselves. The census records for nearby buildings show a high density of people with Sephardic names from "Turkey." The New York community was large enough to allow the luxury of splitting into even smaller divisions based on the town of origin. For example, my father always resented the Jews from Salonica and Rhodes looking down on their hillbilly brethren from the mountains of Monastir. So strong, it was cited in a 1929 report from the Bitolan Jewish community to the Yugoslav national Jewish leadership, this parochialism within the New York community held back the economic progress of the Monastirlis immigrants. In New York, Victor was a member of the Peace and Brotherhood Congregation of Monastir. Started as a synagogue, today it remains as a burial society. Victor's grave is near the center of the burial plot in King David cemetery in Elmont, New York. He's still surrounded by the community of his youth, his parents' community.

We don't know exactly how Victor and Fortune met. Supposedly, Fortune lived with her eldest brother, Bohor, and his family. Bohor was seventeen years older than Fortune, and apparently his wife, Rachel, regarded my grandmother more as a servant than a younger sister. Understandably, Fortune wanted to get out. From their marriage certificate, we know that 25-year-old Victor was already at 135 Orchard Street and that his new 21-year-old wife just moved in with him. When she signed her marriage certificate, Fortune lived at 183 Orchard. So, she must have already moved out of her brother's apartment at number 153. They all lived in the three blocks of Orchard Street between Houston and Delancey Streets. Victor and Fortune might have met on the street. Aunt Beck and my dad both say that he loved her intensely and showed the love much more than she was able. There's also a family story that she fell in love with a "singer" before meeting Victor. The family disapproved. Maybe that was the "beau" she visited in California after Victor's death?

On April 5, 1916, my Aunt Annie, Victor and Fortune's first child, was born. She was named after her late grandmother, Anna Negrin. By June 1917, Victor worked as a factory machinist and electrician. These were both skills he probably learned in the context of agriculture at the farm school in Djédéida. The school had an electrical generation plant, as well as all the facilities necessary to maintain and repair farm equipment.

We know these bits of information from Victor's World War One draft card. Victor registered to fight against the Ottoman Empire of his birth, against the Bulgarians and Germans currently destroying his hometown and shelling his family. He would possibly fight alongside the French culture he learned at the Alliance schools. It must have caused a confusion of emotions. It never came to pass. He had dependents and didn't have to serve alongside his cousin and future brother-in-law, Morris Cassorla. Uncle Morris did his army duty serving in the coastal defense of Rhode Island. He never went overseas.

At the time of Victor's draft registration, Fortune was likely pregnant with Jacob, their second child, the "First Jacob." She probably gave birth in early 1917. In the Sephardic tradition, the child was named to honor

Victor's father. Perhaps this means that Victor and his father were reconciled by this time. We don't know.

The growing family moved to 24 East 114th, a largely Spanish speaking East Harlem neighborhood made up of both Sephardic Jews and people from Puerto Rico. In a scholarly piece about Ladino in New York during the early 1920s, a language scholar named Max Luria tells a story about walking in East Harlem and hearing Spanish in every store. The language was the same. The lettering of the signs was different. In the Sephardic stores, they were written with Hebrew letters. In the Puerto Rican stores, notices were in Latin letters. Later, on a recording, I heard Joe Elias (the musician who was my Uncle Abe's first cousin), say that when his parents came to Harlem, they thought everyone was Jewish because Spanish was being spoken all around them. Victor and Fortune probably felt at home there, although they didn't stay long.

We know that Victor and Fortune's second child, Jacob, was born in early 1917 because of his death certificate dated February 19, 1919. On it, his age is two years old. He died of pneumonia resulting from influenza. For the rest of her life, Fortune blamed the death of Jacob on taking care of her extended family. Up to this point, she apparently tried to take care of everybody. After Jacob died, she maintained a "Better from far away" philosophy. People are mostly OK, just as long as they don't get too close. This is something my father inherited strongly. This philosophy certainly affected our family over the years.

My father never realized his older brother died of the "Spanish Flu" until in the middle of the Covid pandemic, when we carefully read Jacob's death certificate. During this latest pandemic in 2020, the family lost my cousin Madeline, Aunt Annie's daughter. She would have been this Jacob's niece.

When young Jacob died, Fortune was pregnant with her second son, Isaac. Isaac was the name of both Fortune's father and Victor's grandfather. When Isaac came home from the hospital in 1919, the family moved back downtown to 164 Chrystie Street. In 1915, Chrystie Street and its Sephardic coffeehouses were the center of the Sephardic community. By 1920, 164 Chrystie was almost entirely Italian. This might account for my father's memory of his father speaking Italian.

In the hallway leading to my room at my parents' house, there's a formal portrait photograph of Victor, Fortune, and Annie taken in 1920. Annie is about four years old. She's sitting up on a pedestal. Her parents are dressed in their finest. This is the oldest family picture we have of Victor. He's got a round face and a snazzy mustache. I've spent a lot of time looking at this photograph, wondering what the man was like. What I never considered about the portrait was its timing. Where was Isaac?

Isaac is remembered as a golden child. Apparently, Victor couldn't believe he had such a good son. He said that babies must have been switched at the hospital. Isaac soon had some younger siblings, my Uncle Jack, the second Jacob, was born in 1921. My Aunt Beck, named in honor of Fortune's mother, Rebecca, was born in 1923.

August 28, 1926, was a terrible day for my family. The *New York Daily News* reported, "Auto Kills Boy—Isaac Youcha, 7, 67 South 10th Street, Brooklyn died last night from being hit by an automobile." He hit his head on the curb. Fortune took him to the hospital where they waited four hours. In the overcrowded emergency room, Isaac was never seen by a doctor and died in his mother's arms. Victor came home from work to find out that his idyllic son was dead. Writing this almost a hundred years later makes my heart break. Victor and Fortune lost two children in less than 10 years, yet they carried on. Within a few months, Fortune was pregnant with my father, who would also be named Isaac. He was born on the kitchen table at 125 Ludlow Street. There would be no doubt about babies being switched in the hospital.

Aunt Vida

Vida Youcha Cassorla was my Grandfather Victor's younger sister, born in Monastir on August 30th, 1901. She and her husband, Uncle Morris, were my closest living links to Monastir. They died when I was in my teens and twenties, but I never thought to ask them about their lives. I was young and not focused on the personal parts of our family history. What a missed opportunity.

I have many memories of Vida and Morris. Most embarrassingly, I always unknowingly mispronounced her name. I guess the Monastirli accent makes "Vida" sound very much like "Villa," and that's what I called her. No one ever corrected me. Hopefully, she couldn't tell the difference. I remember Aunt Vida and Uncle Morris coming to the house for Passover and Thanksgiving. Uncle Morris would sit in the blue wing chair in the living room with his hat on. Vida would sit on the bench right next to him. She'd talk "at" him, rather than "to" him. He'd close eyes and "go to sleep" as his hat slid over his face. Frustrated, Vida would wave her hands in the air, and go into the kitchen. Morris would then open one eye to make sure the coast was clear and rejoin the conversation. I was very young, maybe four, when I first saw this happen. I remember being surprised. I'd never seen a couple behave like this.

I also remember Vida and Morris sitting around the dining room table talking with Grandma. They were really the ones who spoke Ladino. In a mix of Ladino and English, my dad, with my aunts and uncles, would ask them questions. I remember watching those conversations, but I don't remember much of what was asked, or many specific answers.

I have a vague memory of Morris and Vida's front steps and the kitchen table at their house in Brooklyn. Vida's food was the best in the family, much better than Grandma's or even Aunt Beck's. My mom would tell the story of how when she first joined the family, she wanted to learn to cook traditional Sephardic food for her new husband. Aunt Vida was the best cook in the family, so Vida's house in Bensonhurst was the place to go for cooking lessons. At some point, my mom asked to learn how to make phyllo, the thin pastry dough used for *spinaka* and *burekas*. Aunt Vida said, "You know you can buy this frozen, now?" My mom (being herself) insisted. When she showed up on the appointed morning, the kitchen table was cleared. Aunt Vida took a fist sized lump of dough from the refrigerator, plopped it in the middle of the table and said, "Now, we stretch this (the dough), over this (the table)." I think Mom bought the frozen dough after that.

Morris and Vida went into the Sephardic Home for the Aged in Brooklyn when I was in junior high or the beginning of high school. Uncle Morris was going senile and living back in his Monastirli boyhood. He was happy in the past, but Vida wasn't content in the Home. I remember going there to visit them. I know I didn't really like the place. One time I didn't go to see Vida and Morris at the Home was April 15, 1977.

My mom and dad visited, and my dad recorded part of their conversation on the cassette I later found at my parent's house. Vida and Morris asked after me. Regrettably, I didn't go because I was working stage crew for a high school play.

My dad and Aunt Beck certainly had lots of stories about their "Aunt V." When dad was a little boy and the families lived near each other on the Lower East Side, Vida would take him out for walks. "Why are you always asking so many questions?" My dad was continually curious, and still is. Many other stories about Vida floated through the family. Vida tried to correct how her family in America pronounced our last name. "What is You-Cha? Our name is "You-shah." It was no secret how much Victor loved her, and no secret that my grandmother had problems with Vida. Grandma felt that Morris and Vida looked down on her because she was uneducated. Then there are those stories about Vida's cooking; at 94, my dad still remembers the twirled pattern of her spinach pies.

Morris and Vida Cassorla didn't have any kids. My dad doesn't know if this is because they didn't want them or they couldn't have them. I think the latter. Vida and Morris were first cousins. Vida's mother, Anna Negrin, was the sister of Morris's mom, Tova Negrin. And, since both of Vida's grandmothers were Cassola's, there may be even more of a genetic conflict resulting in infertility.

It seemed a piece of Brooklyn came upstate whenever the family visited my parent's house for Passover or Thanksgiving. Aunt Beck and Uncle Rubie would pick up Grandma and then swing by for Morris and Vida. Grandma would always get carsick during the ride up. I didn't realize how long a trip it was, and how much of an effort everyone made. It was obviously very important for the family to gather.

Before this research, we didn't know if Victor left for Tunisia before Vida was born. We didn't know if her mother, Anna, died as a result of Vida's birth. At some point in her youth in Monastir, Vida didn't have to eat at home. Her father set up an "account" at a local restaurant. She could go in an order whatever she wanted. There obviously wasn't a mother at home cooking for her. My cousins found her immigration documents from May 29, 1921. These confusing and intriguing documents say that Vida was born August 30, 1901, in Monastir. Her last name was listed as

Ioushah. She came to America from Florina, Greece, only 12 miles from Monastir. Vida last stayed with "Uncle Jesoua." Is Jesoua a first name, or a last name? If it's a bad interpretation of Ishach, or Youchah, why is it written on the immigration form differently than her last name? All the questions could just be the legacy of an overworked immigration officer.

The documents in the Alliance Archives straightened out some of the kinks in these stories and enabled us to put them onto a timeline. We now know that Vida had her mother until she was 7 or 8, since Anna Negrin died around 1909. The Alliance documents also tell us that Victor didn't leave Monastir until just after Vida celebrated her second birthday. This helps account for Victor's extreme affection towards his "baby sister." It must have been like the affection Beck still held for my dad, her "baby brudder," when they were both in their 90s.

Left: Uncle Morris and Grandma Talking Ladino. (Youcha family photo from Emily Youcha) Right: 2022 view of Vida and Morris's house in Bensonhurst, Brooklyn. (Zack Youcha photo)

Monastir 1911

Monastir Becomes Bitola

After 500 years, how, and why, did Monastir change its name to Bitola? The answers to those questions go back to the time when Jacob married Bochora and started his second family. Their story fleshed out the bare bones of the area's history and made it personal.

The Alliance records concerning my family seem to end with Jacob's December 17, 1909, letter to Narcisse Leven, where he dramatically says his wife has died and he's contemplating suicide. Rante, our "man in Macedonia" and now a good friend, picked up Jacob's trail in the archives in Bitola. Rante's readings of the notes Jacob Aroesti prepared for his Yizkor memorial book told us that Jacob remarried a woman named Bochora, and that they had two daughters, Roza and Anna. We knew everyone's birth dates. Anna was born in 1914, while Roza was the firstborn in 1912. Given Roza's birthday, it's reasonable to assume that Jacob and Bochora married a year earlier, in 1911, after Jacob learned his son was safe in New York.

How did Aroesti know this level of detailed information? Was he a close friend of the family? In 2021, Rante found the answer. Amongst the yet unprocessed materials in the Bitolan Archives are Serbian registers of the Jewish community of Bitola. Line 2945 on page 42 lists Jacob's family.

The years from Roza's birth in 1912 to my father's birth in 1927 were largely very hard years in Monastir/Bitola. The Young Turk revolution in 1908 turned the Ottoman Empire into a constitutional monarchy. The initial optimism and enthusiasm for the revolutionary ideas and ideals quickly faded. It seems that in many Jews' minds the benefits of citizenship were being outweighed by the burden of military conscription. Young men were constantly leaving Monastir for Europe and the Americas.

Balkan Wars

As *Mouktar,* Jacob's role made him responsible for obtaining the passports of those emigrating Jews, along with overseeing official processes like the census. He likely soon lost those powers as a result of the First Balkan War. This war saw Greece, Bulgaria, Serbia, and Montenegro—"The Balkan League"—attack the Ottoman Empire with the objective of carving up the Empire's remaining European lands. In March 1912, before the war started, Bulgaria agreed with Serbia that Bulgaria would get most of Macedonia, including Monastir. It was all part of a nationalistic "Greater" Bulgarian creation story that depended upon an empire which had its seat in Macedonia and lasted two generations almost 1,000 years earlier.

In 1912, the Bulgarians tried to right what they viewed as a diplomatic wrong committed 34 years earlier. Initially, Russia's 1878 war against the Ottomans gave Macedonia to the new, quasi-independent Bulgaria. Within a year, the Western great powers handed Macedonia back to the Ottomans at the Treaty of Berlin. They didn't want a powerful Russian ally in the Balkans, and they didn't care about the Bulgarian's reactions. The consequences of this decision caused several more wars and horrible destruction in Macedonia.

When the First Balkan War started on October 8, 1912, Bulgaria, with its strong army, pushed the Turks back through Thrace to within 40 miles of Constantinople. One of the main battles in Thrace was at Kir Kilisse, my grandmother Fortune's hometown. The fighting eventually led to her coming to America and meeting Victor. The importance of the battle at Kir Kilisse was even commemorated in Monastir by the Bulgarians during their occupation during World War Two. When we found the address of Jacob Samuel Ishach during our first visit to Bitola, we looked for a street named Lozengrad, the Bulgarian name for Kir Kilisse.

While Bulgaria was quickly rolling through Thrace, Serbia conquered most of Vardar Macedonia. On October 28th, 1912, they took Monastir with a battle that happened north of the city and did little damage to the town. The war was soon over, but the resulting peace didn't last long.

Dictated by the Great Powers of Europe (England, France, Germany, Austria-Hungary, and Russia), the Treaty of London created an independent Albania and gave the Balkan League the rest of Macedonia, as well as a good part of Thrace—to within 80 miles of Constantinople. The treaty didn't specify how the members of the League should divide up Macedonia. It turned out Serbia didn't abide by its prewar agreement with Bulgaria to give up some pieces of conquered Macedonia. To remedy the "injustice," Bulgaria attacked its former allies and started the Second Balkan War. Feeling that they hadn't been properly rewarded for staying out of the First Balkan War, Romania, Bulgaria's northern neighbor, attacked and nearly took the Bulgarian capital, Sofia. Soon, the Turks joined in and attacked Bulgaria, taking back most of Thrace. Basically, Bulgaria miscalculated badly and got its butt kicked. The ramifications of this miscalculation would affect Monastir in both the First and Second World Wars.

The results of the Balkan Wars drastically changed Jacob's world. Not only did 500 years of Ottoman rule end, but Monastir became part of Serbia. Just as Bulgaria's creation story rationalized its possession of Monastir, so did Serbia's. The story of "Greater Serbia" demanded loyalty. There was no room for anything, or anyone, with the least hint of Ottoman, Albanian, Greek, or most certainly Bulgarian heritage. The contemporaneous report by the Carnegie Institute of Peace makes clear that everything needed to be Serbian, including names, schools, and religion. The new rulers even changed the name of the town from Monastir to the more Serb "Bitolj" (Bitola in English), a version of the name it held before the Turks conquest. "Serbianization" turned the small world of Monastir on its head.

A flood of refugees engulfed the town. The Carnegie Institute for Peace's report made immediately after the brutal war compiled horrific statistics. Along with much rape and murder, over eighty percent of the local Muslim villages were burned, and their people scattered. Forty-two hundred Serbian families resettled in their place. Fifty thousand Serbian police came in to keep the peace, as did Serbian priests to keep the faith.

Recognizing the influence of schools in the area, the government made sure that if a student did not attend a Serbian school, the family was fined. Also, all men of the appropriate age served in the Serbian Army, causing even more young Jewish men to leave.

A mountain frontier town, Monastir traded for hundreds of years with the second largest port in the Empire, Salonica. Now, the trading partners were cut off from each other by national borders. Salonica became Greece's Thessaloniki. The loss of trade compounded the economic effects of the war, and along with all the other changes, amplified the emigration of Jews (and others) from Monastir. Their world under the essentially benign neglect of the Ottomans ended; there was now more for them elsewhere than at home.

With the termination of Ottoman authority, Jacob lost his official position as *Mouktar*; his trade, as a moneychanger, or *seraph*, continued, but was apparently tightly regulated. *Seraphim* exchanged foreign currency and made loans for real estate, businesses, weddings, and moving abroad. They also received the remittances sent home by overseas Monastirlis. The changing borders and trade dynamics must have lessened his business, just as they did everyone's in town. Jacob was also apparently cut off from his "house by the sea," which was likely in Salonica. With all these changes and being almost 50 years old, it was a difficult time to start a second family.

A Manaki Brothers' photograph captured the prominent male members of the Jewish community with the head Serbian rabbi, Isaac Alcalay, at the Bitolan train station. Most of the men wore Western dress and hats like the Rabbi. A few wore fezzes. When I first saw it, I hoped that one of those men could be Jacob, but the image was too blurry to tell.

Forty years later, Milton Manaki inscribed the photograph saying that the visit was in 1913, but documents in the Alliance Archives provide a different date. The Director of the Alliance Boys School, Joseph Bensimhon, wrote the Central committee about a March 27, 1914, visit of Rabbi Alcalay; there doesn't seem to be a record of an earlier trip. It was an official visit. The Serbian government paid Rabbi Alcalay's salary. Most likely, his time in Bitola was part of Serbia's efforts to tie the people to the nation through religion.

Dr. Alcalay the Grand Rabbi of Serbia charged by the Minister of Public Instruction and Religions to visit Jewish communities in the Serbian conquered areas and to organize them, arrived in Monastir last Wednesday.

Director Benismhon's account gave a good picture of the changes taking place in the Jewish community resulting from the Balkan Wars. He talked about the steep rise in emigration.

For several years, following the example of the Greeks and Bulgarians, the Jews of Monastir have emigrated to America. Up until now, the departures have been isolated, but since one month there's been a real convoy on the train each day. The idea of escaping military service and [making] their fortune in the New World pushes a large number of the young people to leave the country.

Bensimhon made clear the purpose of the Rabbi's visit: "The Grand Rabbi expressed to me the greatest satisfaction that I've already started the work of reconstruction that's the special objective of this mission." A few months later Director Bensimhon writes the Central Committee saying that the "reconstruction" has not been going well.

On 1 July 1914, Bensimhon reports that the Balkan Wars destroyed the economy of the Jewish Community in Monastir, largely because the

Serbian Rabbi Isaac Alcalay visiting Monastir/Bitola in 1914. Taken at the train station. (Scan from Last album: Keeper of Memories of the Jewish Religious Community, *Alexander Manojlovski)*

new national borders cut off the relationships with trading partners. He also summarizes the Jewish population divided by economic class:

- 168 affluent class. Including 18 money changers. (Jacob was one of these.)
- 133 Middle Class
- 525 Poor Class
- 176 Manual Trades (Listed after the poor!)

The disruption of the Balkan Wars was bad, but it was almost nothing compared to the destruction that came with World War One.

World War One

In the 12 years preceding 1914, Monastir saw a violent revolution with 8,000 people murdered in the area, a peaceful revolution, and a war that ended 500 years of traditional rule. In neighboring Bosnia, the June 28th assassination of Austrian Archduke Franz Ferdinand by a Serbian citizen sparked a war that destroyed Bitola. On July 28th, the Austro-Hungarian Empire declared war on Serbia, Jacob's new country. Germany, Bulgaria, and the Ottoman Empire later joined the war on Austria-Hungary's side and formed the "Central Powers." By the 21st of November 1915, the Bulgarians conquered Bitola as part of their domination of Serbia. Their German allies soon joined them in the occupation. Through a miraculous retreat and evacuation to the Greek island Corfu, the Serbian army survived and regrouped with its French allies in Salonica. A year later the "Allies" attacked in the Balkans and created the "Macedonian Front." On November 19, 1916, Serbian and French troops recaptured Monastir/Bitola. The offensive then stalled. The town remained the frontline.

The Germans and Bulgarians retreated into the mountains with their artillery and started shelling the town. The French responded with their artillery. Both sides used poisoned gas and incendiary shells. Together, the Central and Allied powers destroyed Bitola. It suffered, as did all World War One frontline communities. Photographs of the wreckage and carnage in Bitola could be swapped with pictures from the Western Front in France; no one would know the difference.

If people could leave, they did. By the time the Bulgarians and Germans surrendered in September of 1918, only 500 Jews out of a prewar population of 4,000 remained. Most fled to Florina and Salonica, both in Greece. Florina is only 30 miles from Monastir, a very long day's walk. Salonica is just over 100 miles away. At least a week's walk. There were also trains. I have no idea if they were accessible to refugees. The unlucky people who went to Salonica then experienced the horrible 1917 fire that destroyed the center of town, the Jewish Quarter, and the Port.

Compiled in the 1920s, the Serbian Registry of Bitola's Jewish Community recorded the people then living in town. From this registry we know that six months before the Allies reconquered Bitola, Jacob and Bochora had another daughter they named Anna, likely in honor of my great grandmother, Jacob's first wife, Anna Negrin. What a crazy time to have a baby. I'm writing this as the Russians are bombing Ukrainian towns (March 2022) and there's another senseless war in Europe. Sadly, people don't seem to change much.

Our Family in World War One

Stories about the destruction of their town during World War One were well known to the Monastirli community in New York, but I never heard of any direct family connection—until I found a recording of my father and mother interviewing Aunt Vida and Uncle Morris. During the interview, my father asks about the invasion and then bombing of Bitola. (My dad calls it Monastir.) Aunt Vida replies, but it doesn't seem my folks were listening closely because I never heard this story, and my dad has no memory of it.

Taped on April 15, 1977, at the Sephardic Home for the Aged in Brooklyn, the entire interview is only eleven minutes. It was salvaged off an old cassette and the audio was enhanced digitally. Most of what gets discussed is mundane, about Aunt Vida's back brace and Uncle Morris's declining memory. However, about three to four minutes into the tape, Vida says that she had a younger sister, who was killed by German bombs during World War One when the little girl was four. Vida would have been about 14. Perhaps she helped raise the child as my sister Vicky (who is ten years older than I) helped raise me?

Repeated, careful reviewing of the recording yields the following exchange:

Dad: Were you in Monastir when the Bulgars came?
Morris: I don't remember.
Dad: (to Vida) Were you in Monastir when the Bulgars came?

Vida: In less than two years, three government they changed. The Bulgarians came. French they came. It was how my sister got killed.
Mom: This was the Balkan War?
Vida: This was the First World War. ... The Germans killed my sister.
Dad: With the bombs?
Vida: With the bombs. She was four years old then.

All the documents we found said Jacob and Bochora had two children, Roza and Anna. There's no indication of a third sister, other than this recording. However, Vida clearly says her sister died. The timing works out. The daughter died during the German bombing of Bitola, between November 1916 and August/September 1918. If she was four when killed, the window for her birth is from November 1912 to September 1914. Since Roza was born on November 8, 1912, my guess is that this daughter was born in late 1913 through 1914. Possibly Roza

Bitolan children killed in World War One by a German gas attack. (Courtesy of Ministère de la Culture [France] - Médiathèque de l'architecture et du patrimoine - diffusion RMN)

and she were twins. Finding another family member about which we knew nothing is pretty amazing. It's also tragic for a four-year-old to die, especially that way.

After their little girl's death, Jacob and his family probably joined so many others and left Bitola. We don't know where they went, but we do know a few things from which we can pull some possibilities. Did they move to Florina in Greece and join the other Jews from Bitola who had recently founded the community? If so, who did they live with? There is one clue from Holocaust deportation lists.

As mentioned earlier, when Vida came to New York, her immigration documents listed her last name as Ioushah. Her last place of residence was Florina, where she lived with "Uncle Jesoua." In the Holocaust deportee list for Florina, there are a lot of "Ichaj"s. (Our name gets spelled many ways, given the translation into different languages and alphabets.) One is Abraham Isaac Ishaj aged sixty-three. He was born in 1880 and his father's name was Isaac, just as Jacob's. His wife's name was Bochora, also just like Jacob's. He could have been Jacob's younger brother. We don't know. Again, I feel that Vida knew all this, and I was such a fool not to ask.

Jacob and his family were likely not in Bitola during the 1919/1920 winter. Their names are not on the list of Jews who received clothing sent from their community members in America through the American Jewish Joint Distribution Committee, "The Joint." (This historically valuable list also gives the addresses of the recipients.)

Emigration from Bitola

A report from the Jewish Committee in Bitola for the 1929 national Jewish Almanac says that in 1910, just before the end of Ottoman rule, there were 7,000 Jews in Bitola. At the time of the report, there were only half that number. "It was in 1910 that emigration to North America began. New York has the [most emigrants], followed by Rochester and Indianapolis. The reason for emigration in the above-mentioned areas has always been the poor financial situation of these people. Today in the United States, there are about 4,000 Jews from Bitola." In other words, more Monastirlis were in America than in Monastir.

The report makes clear that the Monastirlis in America didn't all prosper. They kept to themselves and didn't associate with the larger New York Jewish community. They "remained in special neighborhoods and founded special organizations and synagogues" seemingly to their own detriment. In hindsight, this self-isolation had some benefits for the immigrants' descendants. They kept parts of their culture alive.

This happened in my family. My dad says that until he was five and went to New York public school, he might as well have been raised in Monastir. Everything he saw, heard, and ate was Sephardic. My grandfather, Victor, is buried with his fellow Monastirli, in the plot of the "Peace and Brotherhood Society of Monastir." The research of my cousins Linda and Emily show how Victor served as our family's anchor for immigration. In 1913 my Uncle Morris's oldest brother came to New York, sponsored by his cousin, Victor Youchah, then living on Chrystie Street. Later, in 1919 Uncle Morris's widowed mother, Tova, came over followed by her younger children. And, as I've said earlier, my grandfather's sister, my Aunt Vida, came to New York in 1921. My family's experience was not unique. The men usually came first and made enough money to send for the rest of the family. When the women came, they brought much of the culture, especially the food, folklore, and music.

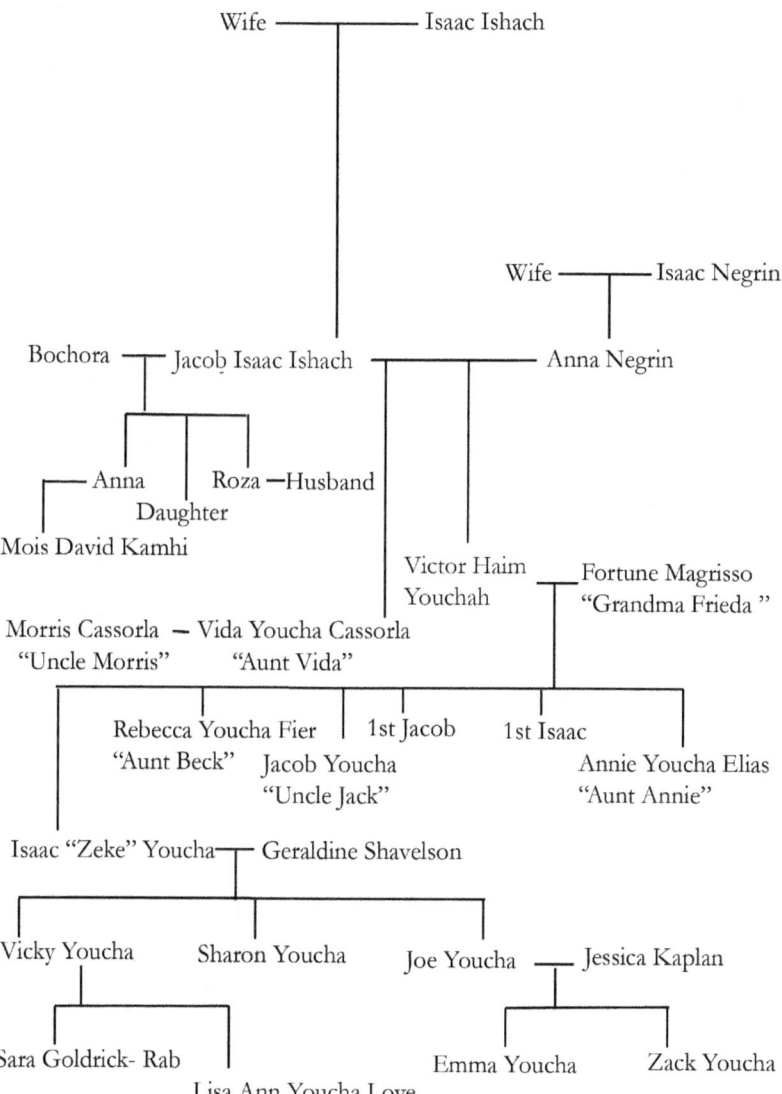

Youcha family tree with Jacob and Bochora's third daughter.

New York 2020

Music From Monastir

Almost all the Monastirli families in the US seemed tied together. Among the leading Rabbinic families of Monastir were the Elias/Cassorlas. There were many brothers. When they came to US Immigration at Ellis Island, half the family kept the name Cassorla, while others took their middle name, Elias. Apparently, the advisors from HIAS (The Hebrew Immigrant Aid Society) felt Elias sounded more Jewish. It's possible that the Youchas were related to these Cassorlas in Monastir; my cousin Emily figured out that both of Victor's grandmothers were Cassorlas. The families are definitely related in America. My Aunt Annie married Abe Elias, Joe Elias's first cousin. Joe Elias the musician founded the Elias Ladino Ensemble. Joe's son, Dan, played at Ladino Day 2020 and now calls Emma "primo" (cousin). Joe's mom was Sarah "Shorty" Cassuto Elias. When Shorty came to America in 1912, she brought along the songs of her youth in Monastir. It's largely these songs that I study with my oud teacher, Ara. Learning Shorty's songs is another story full of coincidences.

At Ladino Day in 2020, when Dan Elias met the Youchas, we had a great time. We talked about family, music, and instruments. Dan gave us a copy of the Elias Ladino Ensemble's CD, *Ladino Lives!* In passing, Dan mentioned that in his mom's basement there were a bunch of ouds acquired by his father over the years. My ears perked up. What if there was an old Jewish oud there? I had no idea if such a thing could exist, but I was certainly interested in finding out! We said we all needed to get together soon. Then, the pandemic hit. It would be over a year before Dan and I met again.

During that time, we'd email and occasionally talk. I became more and more interested in finding songs that would have been sung in Monastir. I remember asking Dan about possible songs. His replied, "There are so many songs, so many songs…" but just left it at that. Meanwhile, I read through Mark Cohen's book again and found a whole section concerning the music of Monastir. Mark relied on the work of Susanna Weich-Shahak, an Israeli musicologist who collected Sephardic songs from the Eastern Balkans. I found some of Susanna's songs available online through the Israeli National Library's sound archives. Listening to the music, watching the videos of Simo and Allegre Calderon, and hearing their conversations in Ladino all brought back memories of hearing my grandmother, Great Aunt Vida, and Uncle Morris talking around my parent's dining room table. I got up my gumption and emailed Susanna to see what else I could learn.

Within a few hours, she responded and provided me with recordings and transcriptions of the lyrics she made of Avram Sadikario singing in the early 1990s. Before World War Two, Avram was a young communist medical student in Bitola. He went on to fight with the Partisans and survived, as did his future wife, Jamilla Kolonomos. Jamilla wrote several of the books I'd gotten at the Holocaust Museum in Skopje in 2018. She documented much of the culture of her youth. I soon learned that Avram and Jamilla were the surrogate grandparents of Goran Sadikario, the Director of Macedonia's Holocaust fund. Like most things involving Sephardic Jews, the people were starting to weave together.

Learning the Oud

This particular story also has an Armenian thread. Over the summer of 2020, I realized that if I wanted to learn the oud, I really needed a teacher. My luthier guru and sometimes oud teacher, David Rapkevian, moved to Maine, and learning from a book wasn't working. I've always believed in getting the best teachers I can. I decided to be bold and ask Ara Dinkjian if he would teach a rank beginner. After all, the oud I built was based on the measurements of one of Ara's Manols… Thankfully, Ara said yes, and I started learning the oud and music theory, as well as vastly broadening my knowledge of Sephardic music.

It wasn't playing a fretless instrument that scared me. It was overcoming all the barriers I'd constructed since I sat at the piano as a young boy, unable to memorize a piece of music and totally intimidated by a metronome. My wife and I both felt that our combined sense of rhythm was so minimal that at the start of the first dance at our wedding we waited for the band to play the intro a second time before we could step properly into "All of Me." On top of the mental hurdles, my left hand would never regain the parts it lost to that joiner accident over forty years ago. Being a good teacher, Ara ignores my barriers and supposed disabilities. He pushes me, sets the path, and very occasionally picks me up.

Ara Dinkjian is an Armenian born in America—northern Jersey to be exact. He's one of the great oud players in the world, and an excellent teacher. Ara uses the oud and his career (really, his life) to preserve Armenian music and build bridges between all the cultures influenced by the oud as it travelled from Persia through the Middle East, the Balkans, and all the way to Spain. Yet, as a platinum selling composer, he writes songs for the present.

Working with Ara opened the world of my family's music. As with most "folk music," it's passed down in an oral tradition. As I studied, I discovered the beauty, sorrow, and fun inherent in the songs and the people who wrote and enjoyed them. There's drinking, sex, God, and joy—all sung in Ladino. Ara's become a friend not only to me, but also my family. When I show up for a lesson alone, he asks, "No dad? No son? No wife? No dog?" His response after my negative reply is, "Oh. Well. Okay." Fortunately, I still get my lesson.

In my pursuit of songs from Monastir, Ara generously agreed to transcribe the music of the songs sung by Avram Sadikario as well as one recommended by Dan Elias. We had about half a dozen songs. I was looking for more. Boy, did I find them.

Down in the Basement

Dan Elias and I reconnected in May of 2021, when he cleaned out his parents' basement. He said there were probably more than half a dozen ouds there, along with a bunch of instruments that needed to be fixed.

He would be there that weekend; could I meet him? I couldn't imagine a place I'd rather be.

Describing the basement Dan Elias inherited from his dad, Joe, I fall back to a friend's metaphor. Monte described being inside the house of a mutual tool collecting friend as being inside a mosaic. You just needed to stand there and concentrate. The more you looked, the more tools would appear. So it was in Joe Elias's basement. I found the 1907 Ottoman oud I dreamed of. I also found what seemed like a lifetime of instruments to repair and get back into playable shape. I found what I hoped would be in the house, but probably the most significant things I saw were hundreds of 78 recordings and many feet of stacked reel-to-reel tapes. When we talked about what could be on the reel-to-reels, Dan mentioned that his father recorded older singers from the Sephardic Home for the Aged in Brooklyn, and how, in the late 1970s, his dad also helped set up a federally funded project through the World Jewish Congress which hired young musicians to go out to the Home and document the Sephardic songs remembered by the residents.

Joe Elias's basement. (Joe Youcha photo)

Dan seemed close to overwhelmed by the whole situation, and I was tremendously interested in finding out what was on those records and tapes. So, I offered my help.

By this time, Ara and I met both personally and virtually for lessons. I tried to combine the in-person lessons with monthly visits to my dad—who only lives 40 minutes from Ara. On one trip north, I met Dan and his partner Sheryl. We photographed all the hundreds of 78 labels. Apparently, Joe ran a regular ad in the Sephardic Home's newsletter saying, "If you have old 78s, I'd be more than happy to take them off your hands." It was quite a collection. Ara was able to tell Dan which ones were rare. Naturally, he bought a few himself. Ara has a collection of over 6,000 78s of Turkish and Armenian music someday destined for the Library of Congress.

After one trip north to visit my dad, Ara, and Dan, I came home to Virginia with a high-quality cassette deck and a briefcase full of cassettes. The cassettes were mostly copies of the field recordings from the Sephardic Home, some early concerts of the Elias Ladino Ensemble, as well as a selection of Sephardic music. Listening to those 20 hours of tapes was a revelation. They progressed from the documentary project's field recordings to educational workshops and concerts given by the Elias Ladino Ensemble. The people came alive. The cassettes spanned enough time that I learned some of the singers' stories. They were mostly women who came to America from the Balkans and Turkey between 1900 and 1924. Now in their 80s or older, they all said their voices weren't what they used to be, but their joy in singing the songs was so obvious, it didn't matter.

On one concert tape, Joe Elias uses Sophie Amara as an example of the power of the music. Known as a true singer with a pure voice, a stroke left her mostly incapacitated. Joe first went into her room just to sing to her and hopefully make her feel better. Soon, she was lifting her head. Not long after, she sang along. The recordings capture her beautifully singing the songs she remembered and apologizing for the quality of her voice! By the time Joe gave that concert, Sophie had passed, but as Joe said, she died as herself.

Through listening to the cassettes, I felt as if I was getting to know Joe Elias a little bit. He seemed like quite a character. Not someone who would be easily stopped. Capturing these songs before they were lost was something that he wanted to get done. Along the way, using the World Jewish Congress funding, Joe enlisted the help of a young singer named Robin Greenstein who obviously also knew how to handle the older Jewish singers.

At the Home, there was a well-known singer who recorded professionally in the US during the 1940s, Victoria Hazzan. Almost larger than life, she always had a "tickle in her throat," or "wasn't feeling just right" whenever Robin asked her to sing. After four months of trying, Robin eventually succeeded. Victoria sat down and sang a list of songs, giving Robin songs, or versions, no one else knew. As with most of the singers, Victoria and her family were from the Turkish part of the Ottoman Empire. No one, except Joe, seemed to be from the Balkans.

As part of the project, Robin compiled a Ladino songbook called *La Serena*, the title of a well-known Sephardic song. Dan gave me a copy of this excellent resource that isn't as widely known as it should be.

After completing the recording/documentation project in 1978, Joe and the Elias Ladino Ensemble gave a concert for the residents of the Sephardic Home. My Uncle Morris and Aunt Vida were likely there. More a community sing-along than a concert. I felt as if I was listening to people recapture a piece of their youth.

Started in the mid-1970s at the suggestion of the Smithsonian's Folklife Center, the Elias Ladino Ensemble is a teaching tool. The group doesn't play for weddings and bar mitzvahs, but rather universities and community centers. Joe also taught classes so others could learn the now documented Ladino songs. And, he kept giving concerts. He kept teaching. Joe originally learned the songs the way they were always taught, as part of an oral tradition. He passed them on that way, although he and Dan did write down a lot of the lyrics.

Listening to the concerts, I quickly realized that the Ensemble didn't have a huge set list, and Joe's "patter" didn't change much. He usually said he'd learned "probably 150 songs from his family." Even given a bit of exaggeration (from the "Pete Seeger of Sephardic Music"), these would be a lot of songs from Monastir—if I could identify them. My next step was to listen to the reel-to-reel tapes. I hoped the key would be there. It was, in the voice of Joe's mother, Sarah "Shorty" Elias.

To play the tapes, Dan bought a very nice used reel-to-reel player. He hadn't set it up because some pieces went missing during the unpacking. On one of my trips north, I brought the stack of reel to reels from his mom's house up to him. It turned out, that morning, when he walked across his living room rug, he felt the missing parts under his feet. Dan is a neat and tidy guy. That rug was vacuumed many times over the previous month. Somehow the parts knew I was coming and showed up in time.

I returned the cassettes and cassette deck and took the reel-to-reel player home with an initial box Dan selected of about likely 20 tapes. We were looking for Shorty. We found her, and more.

There were recordings of family sing-alongs, Joe asking Shorty to sing particular songs, and some of Joe's early Ladino teaching workshops that included singers from the Sephardic Home. I like to make spreadsheets to plan and track my work. I compiled a list of the tapes and their contents and how to digitize them safely. I then made a list of all the songs I thought were sung by Shorty. Through the miracle of the Internet, Dan, my son, Zack, and I listened to the tapes and figured out which ones were really Shorty. Zack and a sound engineer friend of his then took the recordings and digitally cleaned up the sound.

Shorty died in 1964, when Dan was about four years old. He has no memory of hearing her sing. He said it was like listening to a lost legend. He was hearing how his dad learned so many of the songs he grew up playing.

I was looking for songs from Monastir. I knew Joe's father was from the town, and I assumed the same for Shorty. I then learned there was a question within the Elias family whether Shorty was born in Nish, Serbia. Some research on Ancestry.com made it clear that when she came to America, she was coming from Monastir. And, on one of the tapes, she clearly says that she's a "Monastir Girl."

Now, I could make my list of the songs I knew were from Monastir. Through Susanna, I had Avram Sadikario and the Calderons. Through Joe and Dan, I had Shorty. All together I had about 30 songs. Ara transcribed them as I learned them, proof again that this music has always been cross-cultural. I didn't grow up hearing many of these songs, but these songs from Monastir connected. They even helped me overcome my rhythmic challenges. Somehow, more complex 7/8 time made more sense to me than simple 4/4 time. Ara said it's in my blood.

New York 1920s–1930s

Vida, Continued

Growing up, my most direct connection to Monastir was through my Great Aunt Vida and Great Uncle Morris. Vida arrived in New York on May 29, 1921, aboard the ship *Megali Hellas*. She left from Piraeus, Greece, a port of Athens, which is about 300 miles from Florina. Why did she

Morris and Vida in the 1920s. (Youcha family photo)

leave from there? Thessaloniki was only 90 miles away from Florina. Perhaps soon after the First World War and the terrible fire, the port wasn't as active? Vida paid her own passage and with $40 in her pocket was going to meet her brother, Victor, who lived at 177 Chrystie Street.

On September 11, 1923, Vida married her first cousin, Morris Cassorla, who was eight-and-a-half years older than she. Morris left Monastir for the US in 1912, when Vida was nine years old. Tova Cassorla, Morris' mother, and Vida's aunt came over in 1919 and in 1925 lived with the young couple at 101 Allen Street on Manhattan's Lower East Side. A census of that year lists both women as "housewives." They lived in a building with a lot of Sephardim. They still lived there in 1930 when Tova died, but the neighborhood changed to be mostly Eastern European Jews and Italians. By the 1940 census, Morris and Vida moved out to 60th Street in the Bensonhurst section of Brooklyn. They stayed there until the mid-'70s when they moved into the Sephardic Home for the Aged.

A two-story house, 2045 60th Street is divided up into apartments. My dad remembers Morris and Vida lived in the back upstairs unit, and Morris made wine from the 1/16th of an acre vineyard he planted in the tiny backyard. I just remember the front steps and the kitchen. As I'm writing this, the smells come back: spectacular cheese *burekas*, baklava that melted in your mouth, and somehow her *spinaka* tasted better than anyone else's. Aunt Beck, who always stayed in Brooklyn, looked after them as they got older, as she did her mother. Vida and Morris's neighbors and close friends also looked after them. My dad says that when Vida and Morris died, the neighbors ended up with most of their things. I wonder if the letter telling of Jacob's death ended up with Vida?

Victor was very close to his sister, and Morris got Victor his last job pressing clothes as part of the Amalgamated Clothing Workers of America. After Victor died, I think Vida and Morris only saw the Youcha side of the family on holidays—aside from Aunt Beck. According to my dad, Morris and Vida associated more with the Cassorla and Negrin sides of the family that made it to New York.

As I said earlier, the main times I saw Morris and Vida were on Thanksgiving or Passover. To be fair, it doesn't sound like my grandmother made them feel welcome. And, my dad felt that, even though he loved his aunt, his mother made him "pick sides." Distance between family members isn't uncommon amongst Monastirlis. There was a joke that at my Aunt Annie's and Uncle Abe's wedding there were 40 people and 10 tables because so few people were talking with one another. I'm also just realizing that the holiday invites and visits were made because of Vida's relationship with Victor, even 30 and 40 years after he died. Like many families, mine's a strange combination of love and antagonism.

Victor in New York, the 1920s and '30s

I've always heard from my father that Victor's favorite job was running a luncheonette on 23rd Street in Manhattan. He was the counterman, the "front of the house," and loved using his language skills to talk with everyone who came in. During his Alliance schooling, the records show that he probably studied French, Hebrew, Turkish, Greek, and Bulgarian in Monastir. In Djédéida, he likely added Arabic and English. His mother tongue, or kitchen language, was Ladino, Judeo-Spanish.

My dad remembers sitting at the counter and watching his father work. He was especially happy when the local French priests came in. They would talk French while he served them food. That's pretty much the family memories of Victor's favorite job. A little research yielded a lot more information.

The Polk's Business Directory for 1933 Manhattan gives the "Youcha Safiha" luncheonette's address as 107 W. 23rd Street. From the Directory we also learn that Victor's partner was Jack Sefiha. We don't know exactly when and how the business began, but it looks like Victor may have started the business and then brought Jack into it. The 1930 census has Victor working at the luncheonette, while Jack is a still a fruit peddler. This census tells us that Jack is a Sephardic Jew from Salonica and about ten years younger than Victor. We also learn Jack is married to Sarah, who came from Izmir/Smyrna, and they have three kids.

In 1930, Victor lived at 51 Malta Street in the New Lots section of Brooklyn where many Sephardic Jews moved. The 1933 business directory lists 371 Hegeman Avenue as his residence, a 2-minute walk from Malta Street. Soon after, the family moved to Neptune Avenue in Brighton Beach, Brooklyn, only a few blocks from the ocean. My dad remembers taking his shoes off at the end of the school year and not putting them back on until he had to go back to class in September. He played on the beach every day. His feet got like leather, and his skin turned dark brown. He loved it. It seems the whole family liked living there. My dad's nearest cousin, Albert Altabet, wrote about visiting the family for a couple of weeks during the summer. Compared to where he lived on Delancy Street, it was like going to the country.

"Victor Youcha and his wife Frieda, my aunt and uncle from the Magrisso side of the family, were of modest means, and yet they took me into their home in the summer. I thought they were rich in a most exceptional way. They were a cheerful family. They made me feel like I was one of the clan which included Anne, Jack, Rebecca and my peer cousin Isaac (Zeke)… They had more than their share of problems during the depression years, yet they were full of life and my stay there was most memorable. [We walked] to the beach in our bathing suits daily. I spent hours diving into the waves. When I got home, my mother called me "Preto" (black)."

It may have been fun at the beach, but it was still the Great Depression. By 1933, Victor may have needed a partner/ investor to make the business work. That's probably why he brought Jack in as a partner. The business lasted until around the beginning of 1940. The census of that year has Victor listed as a restaurant "proprietor," while Jack lists his work as "counterman." It's important to realize that since census takers interviewed people at their residences, they probably talked to the men's wives. This gives us a snapshot of the families' view of their work.

According to family story, this perspective reflects a tension that broke up the partnership after it survived the Depression. My dad always told the story that Victor and Jack ended the business because Jack's wife, Sarah, was "jealous." She thought that Jack wasn't getting his fair share of the business revenue and Victor cheated him. How else could the Youcha family afford to live out by the beach? Putting aside that I'm Victor's grandson, I find this hard to believe. This is the man who wouldn't collect a twenty-year-old loan to a friend.

Regardless, soon after the 1940 census, the partnership dissolved and the luncheonette closed. Victor started a feta cheese business in upstate New York.

Max Luria

One of the first books I looked at specifically about the Jews of Monastir was *A Study of the Monastir Dialect* by Max Luria, a language professor who became interested in the Ladino he heard in New York. The descendant of an illustrious Sephardic rabbinic family and getting his doctorate in philology from Columbia University in 1927, Luria's thesis was on Ladino. The large influx of Ladino-speaking Sephardim from communities in the Balkans, Greece, and Turkey kept the language alive and well in New York. In a piece about the Ladino being spoken in New York, Luria tells that great story about walking in East Harlem and hearing Spanish in every Puerto Rican and Jewish store. I've read the same type of story about Sephardic immigrants arriving in Spanish speaking countries.

Luria's initial research showed him that the people from Monastir, the Monastirlis, spoke the most untouched "original" version of the language. Luria's theory stated that the isolated mountain town retained the uncorrupted language. However, in New York, the Monastirlis were teased by other Sephardim for speaking like hicks using old words and a strange accent. Rather than be singled out, the Monastirlis adopted the more common Ladino usages when out in public. For Luria, it was already too late in New York. If he wanted to find a purer dialect of Ladino, he had to go to Monastir. He did so from July through August 1927.

During his trip, Luria documented folk tales and songs, as well as vocabulary and dialect. His subjects were older men. The women either stayed secluded, or were excluded, from his work. Luria captured a snapshot of the community as it recovered from the Balkan wars and World War One.

Sometime in the 1980s, my dad found a couple of unbound copies of Luria's thesis. They were usually in the stack of books on the table whenever he was studying Ladino. He gave me one of his copies. After returning from our 2018 trip to the Balkans, I had the book bound to protect it. I also started doing some research into Luria. He ended up a professor at Brooklyn College. His papers are at Yeshiva University. Before he died in 1966, he recognized that his and others' research into Ladino captured not only a language, it documented communities that were now destroyed. He started to create an encyclopedia to memorialize those communities but never finished.

While combing the Internet for information about Luria, I learned that the Austrian sound archives preserved his recordings from Monastir and now offered CDs with a very informative accompanying booklet. A mentor of Luria's ran that sound archive and provided Luria with the recording equipment. This seems the likely reason why he deposited the recordings there. They miraculously survived World War Two bombings, and then were conserved in the 1960s. When I received the CD, I expected to hear the voices of the old people whose folktales Luria documented. Instead, I found out that Luria's 1920s recording equipment required strong voices, and that he enlisted two younger men to talk into the microphone, Moise Calderon and Leon Kamhi.

This must be the same Leon Kamhi I read about in all the histories about Jewish Monastir. Playing the CD for the first time, I realized I was hearing the voice of a man central to the history of Monastir between the wars. This voice, from this time (the late 1920s), was the same voice that my great grandfather must have heard many times.

Bitola 1920s–1930s

Leon Kamhi

Leon Kamhi keeps turning up in my family's story. He knew my great grandfather Jacob, and tried to help him emigrate to Palestine, or "make Aliyah," in 1929. He wrote the history of the Jewish community in Monastir/Bitola that mentions the experience of my grandfather going to agricultural school and then Canada. And, he was integral to Max Luria's field work in Monastir.

Kamhi was born in 1898, ten years after my grandfather. In the history of the town, those were a critical ten years. By the time of Kamhi's bar mitzvah at 13, Monastir was no longer part of the Ottoman Empire. By the time he was 20, his town had barely survived World War One, and the British signed the Balfour Declaration promising the Jews a nation in Palestine. Everywhere around him the former Ottoman minorities, Serbs, Bulgars, and Greeks established their own nations. Kamhi strongly believed that the Jews should also have their own homeland.

Educated by the Alliance, and from a wealthy well-connected family, Kamhi spent his life trying to get his fellow Monastirlis settled in Palestine. He sacrificed his personal affairs and business to make this happen in the decades before World War Two. He felt that he needed to be the last to leave; there was no one else to take over his leadership role. This belief cost not only his life but the lives of his young family.

Kamhi made powerful impressions on people. Hundreds of Monastirlis and their descendants have felt that they owe their existence to Leon Kamhi. His childhood friend Louis Rousso immigrated to New York and became very successful in the garment industry. When asked to help fund a memorial to Kamhi, Rousso decided that a book would be better than a statue. Uri Oren's *A Town Called Monastir* was the result. It's the first book I read as a kid about Monastir—although given my interests at the time, I probably didn't finish the book.

(As a side note, in conversation with my dad I learned that around 1912, my great grandfather supposedly arranged for passports for Rousso and helped pay his passage. My dad says his father always had "a warm place in his heart" for the Roussos. During this research, I've also become friends with Louis Rousso's grandson, David.)

While not a great literary work, through extensive quotes and excerpts, Oren's book captures Kamhi's voice. The man wrote constantly, documenting his work in the community while corresponding with different Jewish and government agencies. And, because of his place in the community, people kept his correspondence. Kamhi's note to Ovadia Hazzan asking for his help in resettling my great grandfather and his family likely was kept in personal, family papers. (The Zionist Archives in Israel has no record of the application. There are other archives that might. I still need to check.)

Writing in the 1960s, Oren interviewed the many people in Israel who remembered, and loved, Kamhi. The man truly believed that Zionism and being part of the founding of a Jewish state provided the best future for Monastirlis Jews. For the hundreds of Monastirlis he helped send to Palestine, he was right. He sent them any way he could: by obtaining an inordinate percentage of the British immigration permits allocated to Yugoslavia, by combining families to maximize the effect of each permit, by using tourist visas to send young women who could marry once in Palestine and stay. He helped send well over ten percent of Monastir's post World War One population to Palestine. This was especially vital once the US shut its doors to most immigration in 1924.

Leon Kamhi also worked with the youths of the town, using Zionism to keep them focused on a productive future. It seems that if you were a young person with any type of ambition in Bitola during the '20s and '30s, you were either a Zionist or a Communist. There just wasn't a visible future in Bitola for young Jews. The Zionists believed that there wasn't a place for them in the country's existing power system. The Communists wanted to change the system.

Kamhi's presence in my research even reaches into the music. The voices that Susana Weich-Shahak recorded in Israel singing the songs of Monastir are the voices of people likely saved by Kamhi, who helped them get to Palestine.

Jacob in the 1930s

References in Shlomo Alboher's *The Jews of Monastir*, the Serbian Registry of the Jewish community, as well as Jacob Aroesti's notes for his Yizkor book, tell us about Jacob and Bochora's daughters, Roza and Anna. Roza married and moved to Greece, while Anna married David Mois Kamhi and stayed in Bitola. The couple probably lived around the corner from her parents. At least this is where they were when they were deported in 1943. (There may also be more relevant information in the Serbian registry of the Jewish community. More research will tell us.)

During the 1920s and '30s, Jacob sent gifts to Victor and his family. One question I asked myself when I started the research was, "Why did Jacob stay?" As I've learned more, I think I understand a little bit. Kamhi's note tells us that Jacob obviously considered leaving in 1929. By that time, the United States largely closed off immigration. Jacob had enough money, 500 pounds per person, to avoid the immigration permit "lottery" instituted by the British to enter Palestine. My guess as to why he didn't emigrate to Palestine combines events there with the simple passing of time. The anti-Jewish riots by the Arabs in Hebron may have put off for a few years his desire to go to Palestine. On top of that, by the end of 1929, the Great Depression was in full swing. By 1930, his daughter, Roza, at eighteen was of marriageable age. In contrast, her father was an old man. In 1935, Jacob was 70, not an easy age to leave an established existence. In 1929, he probably thought about leaving for his daughters' futures. By marrying, and in Roza's case moving away, they decided their own.

In the 1942 Manaki photograph for the Bulgarian police registry, Jacob seems a dying man. We don't know how long this had been going on or what was wrong. If he was ill, they wouldn't try to move.

The Head Rabbi in 1930s Bitola, Avram Romano, wrote articles for the Yugoslav Jewish press describing the harsh conditions in the town. He hoped for both aid and a greater share of the Yugoslav permits to emigrate to Palestine. Reports from the local Jewish committee to the national committee in Zagreb make clear that a young person's future was not in Bitola; good jobs just weren't there. The future was elsewhere—either in the Americas or in Palestine. Naturally, the person writing these reports from Bitola was Leon Kamhi.

Leon Kamhi in the center of a Bitolan Jewish youth group. (Cover of Bitolan booklet commemorating the Jewish community—Joe Youcha photo)

Bitola
1941–1943

The Holocaust in Bitola and Our Family

"The Holocaust isn't the beginning of the story, and it's not the end of the story."—Goran Sadikario, Director, Macedonian Holocaust Fund

Like so many European Jewish communities, Monastir's story is one of both Diaspora and Holocaust. As a kid, I focused on the Diaspora. It was easier. It was why I grew up in New York. I always stayed away from thinking about the Holocaust's impact on my family. I rationalized that "everybody" on my mother's side made it to America or England, and that no one stayed in what is now Belarus. And, I knew that in my father's family, Aunt Vida, my grandfather's "only" sister made it to New York.

I never comprehensively applied the history of the Holocaust to my family. I didn't look further than the stories I heard from my dad. We knew Jacob had a second family. We didn't know what happened to them. My dad read something that mentioned a Youchah living in France. He always hoped that they were somehow the second family, but he never looked. Just like he never asked Aunt Vida if she knew what happened to the family that stayed. It was too painful. I think I inherited that attitude, until I started digging into the story in my late fifties. Intellectually, I knew my great grandfather and his second family must have suffered, and likely perished, but I never investigated.

I didn't visit the Holocaust Museum in Washington, DC, until twenty years after it opened. I live less than ten miles away, and my wife's mother and sister volunteered there for years. I just didn't go. I couldn't face it. I knew of the museum's work, especially training police to make sure that "never again" applied in our own communities, but I never went. I saw the exhibits of Yad Vashem in Israel and the Holocaust Museum in Skopje before I looked in my own backyard.

When Jessica and I did visit, it was tremendously powerful. It was also obvious that they weren't telling my family's story. The Museum's exhibits drive home a lesson the world will always need to know, yet they almost ignore the destruction of Balkan Jewry. Even though it's often said that no town in the Holocaust had a higher percentage of its Jews murdered than Bitola, I don't remember it being mentioned. I found the exhibits out-of-date compared to the Museum's research and collections. Hopefully, the interpretive displays will catch up.

I soon visited the Museum again. This time I went to the fifth-floor archives and library. I met a very helpful librarian who steered me towards the books in English and French about the Holocaust in Macedonia. This was when I uncovered a better version of Jacob's Bulgarian Police Registry entry and started studying what I found out later to be the Manaki's photos.

Back at home, I kept looking through the Museum's online photo collection. I found the pictures of Jacob's second wife, Bochora, their daughter, Anna, and her husband, Mois. Bochora is small. Much smaller than her daughter, who bears a strong resemblance to her half-sister, my great aunt Vida. Mois has a glass eye. How did that happen? He looks cheerful, as does Hannah. Nobody is sullen (except for maybe Bochora). I think it's safe to say that they all knew the photographer and felt at ease with him as part of their community.

At first glance, the photos of Mois, Anna, and Bochora look like a group shot that was then cut up for photos of the individuals. Originally, I thought that Mois, Anna, and Bochora were the group. After looking closely at many photos in the Museum's collection, I saw that most were taken in front of the same background. A close look at the backgrounds in Jacob and Bochora's 1942 photos reveals they were sitting next to one another when they sat for Milton Manaki.

Seeing the faces in Manaki's 1942 photos of the Jews in the Bulgarian Police Registry, it's hard to imagine they're all gone, murdered. The Holocaust killed the Jewish community located in Bitola. To use a grim analogy, the Balkan Wars and World War One knocked the community to the ground and kicked it in the face. The interwar years saw it get back on its knees, when World War Two strangled it to death and burned its body. All that was left was a bare outline on the ground and the children who left home before the end.

The timeline of what happened in Bitola during the Holocaust is well documented and seems almost inevitable in hindsight. It's important to remember that it didn't feel that way to the people in the community as these events happened. In fact, I imagine that the ultimate outcome was inconceivable.

Leading up to World War Two, Yugoslavia's Regent, Prince Paul, tended to side with the Fascists, as did Tsar Boris II of Bulgaria. It was certainly the way the wind was blowing in Europe. The government enacted anti-Semitic legislation amidst much internal disruption. In the spring of 1941 both Yugoslavia and Bulgaria signed alliances with Germany and its fellow Fascists. Less than a week after signing that treaty, a group of air force officers deposed the Yugoslav government, and the country declared for the Allies. This did not sit well with Hitler. Already preparing to attack Greece and bail out his Italian ally Mussolini whose invasion of the country stalled, Hitler decided to conquer Yugoslavia on the way.

The Germans captured Bitola on April 9, 1941. Within weeks, the Fascists partitioned Yugoslavia between them. Bulgaria occupied Bitola. Soon after, all the Jews were moved to the north side of the Dragor River into the old Jewish neighborhood, creating a ghetto. The Bulgarians also put laws in place saying that Jews couldn't come to the market before 10 a.m.—putting many out of business.

On August 26, 1942, the Bulgarian Government created the "Commission of Jewish Affairs" and soon created a "Jewish Community Fund" which foreclosed on Jewish properties and bank accounts. To facilitate the robbery, the Bulgarians made the Jews list all their assets and deposit all their money into the Bulgarian State Bank. The Bulgarians then overvalued the assets and assessed a tax that was the actual value of the assets, or greater. Conveniently, all the Jewish money was already "in the bank" and able to be frozen until the taxes were paid.

The United States Holocaust Memorial Museum's (USHMM) library, photo archives, and scholars provided tremendous help and information. Emil Kerenji a research scholar at the USHMM and a friend of my sister-in-law, pointed me in the right direction several times. Most importantly, he connected me to Steven Sage, who has a wealth of knowledge about the Bulgarians, their role in the Holocaust, and the fate of Jews under their control. I owe the level of detailed knowledge concerning the end of the Jewish Community in Bitola to him. Steven provided documents with such detailed information about the fate of my family that I felt physically ill.

I first heard about Steven through Rante, who saw a piece on a Macedonian news website about "Torahs" discovered in the Bitolan Archive, and the involvement of an American researcher. In October 2019, Steven spent about a week in Bitola focusing on the state archives there for the World Jewish Restitution Organization, a constituent of the Jewish Claims Conference which helps negotiate compensation and restitution for victims of the Holocaust and their heirs. Steven works on documenting the theft of cultural properties, including religious texts and objects, along with books and musical instruments. Other areas of interest include

Jacob's house at 60 Neofit Bozveli. (Photo by Beno Ruso. Courtesy of Centropa)

investigating the confiscation of assets such as bank accounts, gold, and jewelry, as well as the takeover of businesses. Steven found the archivists in Bitola very cooperative. In return, he helped them identify certain items in their collection. Steven and I talked about available resources. It seemed we knew all the same people.

Steven told me about an interesting way of identifying Jewish houses by finding *mezzuzot* holes in their doorways. A small case containing the fundamental Jewish prayer "Hear, O Israel, the Lord (is) our God, the Lord is One", a *mezuzah* is attached to a Jewish home's doorpost to fulfill a biblical commandment. They are usually placed at about eye height on an angle, leaving distinctive nail holes.

The Fascists usually forced Jews in a community to live in a small, crowded neighborhood. Steven told me how Bitola was one of the very few places where the Fascists themselves used the word "Ghetto." This is a piece of the story that always stuck with me. The Ottomans let the Jews live where they liked, and where they could afford. Then in 1942 the Bulgarians "relocated" them. The Bulgarians registered my great grandfather at 60 Neofit Bozveli, but that was after (I'm assuming) they relocated everybody. The Ruso family lived in the same house at that time. One of the Ruso sons, Beno, fought as a partisan, survived the war, and became a Yugolsav general. His oral history gives a good picture of life in Bitola before the Second World War. Since starting this research, I've really wanted to know where, and how, Jacob lived before the Holocaust. I think that's why I was so interested in the maps and Bulgarian tax documents.

Steven asked if my family would want to file a reparations claim. I'd never really thought about it and had no urge to do so. It was way more important to me that the story gets told. There are lots of places where the lessons could be applied. We certainly have race hatred in this country, and watching the Christian and Islamic elements of current Macedonian society, it's obvious that the destruction of their Jews eighty years ago didn't teach them enough. I thought pursuing reparations money might get in the way of that work.

Steven checked his documents for Jacob Isaac and the family, particularly the tax records and the record of the roundup and the deportations from Bitola, which was "detailed and vivid." He found Jacob.

The Bulgarian tax assessment document says that Jacob owed 57,707 Bulgarian Leva (the equivalent of about $700 1943 USD; about $12,000 in 2022 USD). The occupying government only levied the tax on Jews. Steven thinks the list was made after the deportations and the taxes were collected after the Jews were murdered.

Small things bring out the horror of the Holocaust. In the Bulgarian Police registry and the German deportation documents, the Jews of Bitola listed their occupations. I wondered why, and Steven made the reason clear. It's probably one of the most purposefully awful things I can imagine. The Jews, my great grandfather, his neighbors, and family, listed their occupations so that they could be best placed in their "new work" in Poland. They were being sent to Treblinka, a camp only meant for immediate murder. The Germans knew this, as did the Bulgarians who signed the "contract" committing these people to death. There was to be no hope. Why offer it?

Using Jacob Aroesti's notes and the German deportation which lists Bochora living with Anna and her husband, Mois David Kamhi, Steven found detailed information that gives a window into my family's last day in Bitola. Here's what Steven said in his email.

> Document BE3a540.jpg is the first page of a two-page document, titled "Protocol," and again listing sums of cash taken from the victims. It's a record of baggage search and confiscation by the ad hoc commission of the Bitola branch of the Bulgarian Commissariat of Jewish Affairs (KEV). The victims on the list are divided among "wagons," i.e., railway cars. This circumstance strongly suggests that the sums recorded on the list were compiled when the victims had already been transported under guard to the Bitola train station but before boarding the trains bound for Skopje where they would be incarcerated in the Monopol tobacco warehouse to await deportation. The list itself, in its present form, was typed the next day for the record, relying on the ad hoc commission's notes as recorded on the spot on March 11. As you can see, the total sums of confiscated cash are tallied for each railway wagon. Also it appears that the victims named

Bulgarian KEV Tax Document listing Jews and their posessions by Rail Car. (Courtesy of Macedonian National Archives, Bitola) here were all heads of household, traveling together with other family/household members who are not named but who were no doubt also thoroughly searched for cash (and valuables).

The next page, Document BE3b541.jpg is the second page of the two-page document, signed by the confiscation commission on March 12. It is on this page that the name Моис Камхи appears, referring no doubt to Mois D(avid) Kamhi whose name is on both the German version of the deportation list and on the Bulgarian deportation list. On the Bulgarian version of the deportation list there is a notation next to the address 54 Neofit Bozveli for Моис Давид Камхи, stating "няма го вкъщи на този" (nyama go vkŭshti na tozi) meaning "not at this house." I interpret that to mean he was registered at 54 Neofit Bozveli but was not physically present there at the time of the arrests on 11 March 1943. Had he separated from his wife, Hana Mois Kamhi? Or had he attempted to hide, or get away? But he was arrested anyway, fleeced of the 1,500 leva in cash he was carrying, and placed onto Wagon #4 of the Skopje-bound train.

… We might also speculate that the two women were also assigned to Wagon #4 for the transport to Skopje, but that cannot be confirmed from this document.

At the bottom of the list there is a total sum for the cash taken from the victims on this train. The total notes how many 200 leva, 250 leva, 500 leva, and 1000 leva banknotes were seized, adding up to 72,450 leva for the whole train, equivalent to about US $883. Here I'll observe the contradiction between the robbery by the authorities and their cover story for the deportation. The victims were told that they were to be resettled somewhere within the old (1940) frontiers of Bulgaria. They would presumably need Bulgarian cash at their new destination, in Bulgaria, but at Bitola they were being robbed of even modest sums of pocket money. The cash confiscations at the Bitola train station thus vitiated the whole cover story.

What Kind of Past 157

The page from Milton Manaki's album of the deported Bitolan Jews which includes Anna, Mois and Bochora. (Courtesy of USHMM)

Close up of Anna, Mois, and Bochora from Milton Manaki's album of the deported Bitolan Jews. (Courtesy of USHMM)

The rubble of Kal Aragon synagogue at the end of World War Two. (Reteived from French Wikipedia article on Jews of Bitola)

Manaki Photo of the Inside of Kal Aragon. (Courtesy of Macedonian National Archives, Bitola)

These 1943 documents really bring the insanity of humankind into focus. Who would document petty theft from people about to be murdered? Steven answers:

> On one hand the Bulgarian Commissariat of Jewish Affairs (KEV) chief (Commissar Aleksandŭr Belev) sought to keep secret the fact that the Jews were being deported to their deaths, so in keeping with Nazi practice the deportations were always referred to in government documents as "resettlement." On the other hand, the KEV mandate was to extract as much wealth as possible from the Jews before transferring them into Nazi German custody.
>
> Even middle and lower ranking KEV functionaries were not supposed to know that deportation meant murder, but the contradictions must have been obvious especially to such personnel who carried out tasks like the confiscation of pocket change (and worse, especially at Skopje and Shtip). The cops and bureaucrats who implemented the fleecing and the deportations probably didn't want to think of themselves as accessories to murder, especially the murder of young children. And so under these conditions a protocol of euphemism and verbal taboo could take hold, something we might describe as "don't ask, don't tell."
>
> The lingering effects of that culture of taboo are detectable even two years later, in March 1945 in the testimonies of Bulgarian witnesses at Sofia People's Court Panel VII, the trial of Bulgarian perpetrators from KEV, the Army, and some civilian institutions. As of March 1943 many people might have suspected that the Jews faced a mortal fate, but people also knew that they weren't supposed to be discussing such things. And so documenting the problem, "What did they know and when did they know it?" turns out to be a very difficult task for the historian working with contemporary, primary source archival materials.
>
> There are only hints, here and there, from the time of the deportations in 1943 and subsequent months.

Thoughts about the Holocaust

Most Jewish families descended from Jews who left Europe before the Holocaust tell similar tales about members that stayed behind and were murdered. The existence of so many doesn't lessen the importance of anyone. The future depends on individuals learning from these stories. Each family must remember and keep teaching future generations.

As Goran Sadikario says, "The Holocaust isn't the beginning of the story, and it's not the end of the story."

Demitir Pechev

"Citizen." "Nation." The movements and realities represented by these terms include liberty and oppression. Whether these terms are viewed positively, or negatively, depends upon how they are applied to people. Usually, Balkan Jews were on the wrong side.

Over and over during our 2018 trip, we saw how citizenship and nationality determined the fate of the Balkans' Jews. In World War Two, Bulgaria was a Fascist ally of Nazi Germany. As a reward for this alliance, Bulgaria acquired territory from both Romania and Serbian Macedonia, which they regarded as historically Bulgarian. Bulgaria also then passed anti-Semitic laws similar to those in Germany. Amongst other things, those laws forbid Jews in conquered territories from becoming citizens. There were now two classes of Bulgarian Jews, those who were citizens and those who were not. The Jews in the newly acquired, formerly Romanian territory, were lucky. The timing saved their lives. The transfer of land happened before the passing of the anti-Semitic laws. Those Jews were citizens. As non-citizens, my family, and approximately 11,000 other Macedonian Jews, died at Treblinka.

It's a dramatic story. As with all stories in the Balkans, this one gets told with different emphasis by different people, largely according to their nationality and beliefs. The basic facts are:

- The Bulgarians made a contract with the Germans to supply them with 20,000 deported Jews.
- There were only 14,000 Jews who weren't citizens, and therefore eligible for deportation, in territories occupied by Bulgaria.

- The Bulgarian in charge of deportation, Belev, arranged to deport the balance of 6,000 Jewish souls from the Jewish populations of several Bulgarian towns. These Jews were Bulgarian citizens.

One of these towns was Kyustendil, where the Jews got word of their impending deportation, apparently the rail cars were already in position. They met with their local gentile neighbors, some of whom went to the capital Sofia to lobby their representative Demitir Pechev, Deputy Speaker of the National Assembly.

Even though he held a powerful position in a Fascist state, Pechev realized the deportation and murder of Bulgaria's Jews would be a stain on the nation. He lobbied his fellow legislators and called in the help of the Metropolitan of the Bulgarian church. Pechev strong-armed the Interior Minister into stopping the next day's deportation of his Jews from Kyustendil, as well as the other Jews who were Bulgarian citizens.

Pechev's life illustrates some of the complexities of the Balkans. Certainly, an interesting man, in World War One, he served as a military liaison to the Ottoman army, the same army Bulgaria fought two years earlier, of the same country that "enslaved" the Bulgarians for over 400 years. As Deputy Speaker of the Assembly in a Fascist state, Pechev was obviously a good party man. His actions and those of his allies saved the lives of about 48,000 Bulgarian Jews. The government persecuted him and stripped all his power. When the Soviets conquered Bulgaria, they imprisoned Pechev as a Fascist. He is, however, acknowledged as one of the "Righteous" by Israel. Our tour leader, Joseph, owes Pechev and the others who helped, his and his family's lives.

Not the Macedonian Jews. They were deported and murdered at Treblinka under the pretext of not being Bulgarian citizens. Learning the details of this lethal bureaucratic farce drove home both the stupidity and importance of national citizenship.

Rabbi Alcalay

One Yugoslav Jew who escaped the Nazis was Rabbi Isaac Alcalay, a very interesting man who connects three generations of my father's family. My great grandfather, grandfather, and father all knew him. His story sheds light on parts of my family's story. Growing up, when my father's family would gather, I'd hear his name all the time. In the New York Sephardic community, he was a legend. In many ways, he established the organized Sephardic community in America. At the end of his life, in the 1970s, he lived at the Sephardic Home for the Aged in Brooklyn, New York. I don't think I ever met him when I visited, but I knew my parents interviewed him before he died. And my dad talked about how, as a young man, he would "raise money for Rabbi Alcalay."

In four years of research, I learned a lot more about the Rabbi. Initially, I found a recording of my parents' interview with him. It was on the opposite side of the cassette tape from their conversation with Aunt Vida and Uncle Morris at the Sephardic Home. I think it was made on the same day. Listening to the interview, I learned about his time as Chief

Rabbi Alcalay from about 1920 (Courtesy of Yeshiva University Archives)

Rabbi of Yugoslavia and his visit to Monastir right after the Balkan Wars. The 1914 Manaki picture from the train station confirms this. The rabbi went on to serve in the Yugoslav parliament, escape after the German invasion in World War Two, come through Palestine to New York and serve as Yugoslavia's representative to America during the war. After the war, he established the Sephardic Jewish Community of America. (That's probably what my dad raised money for, and there's a family picture of my grandmother sitting at a middle table for one of the fundraising dinners. Aunt Vida and Uncle Morris are further back in the room.) On their side of the cassette, when Vida and Morris talk about going to a Passover seder at the Home for the Aged, you can hear the tone in their voices change when they say that Rabbi Alcalay presided over the service. It was a big deal.

I can't find a full biography of him. An obviously remarkable man, he was beloved in the community. The story of his escape from the Germans almost defies belief. As Chief Rabbi in Yugoslavia, he was the most wanted Jew in Belgrade, the first city in the Nazi Reich to be

Rabbi Alcalay circa 1914. (Courtesy of Macedonian National Archives, Bitola)

The US Jewish newspaper with an article about Rabbi Alcalay's escape from Yugoslavia. (Retreived from National Library of Israel)

declared *"judenfrei,"* free of Jews. All the Jews in the city were murdered or deported. Somehow Rabbi Alcalay escaped with his wife and daughter. In the interview with my parents, he says that Christian farmers hid them and saved their lives.

After listening many times to my parents' interview with the rabbi, I wondered exactly how he escaped. I found my answer in 1943 articles from the *Jerusalem Post* and a US Jewish newspaper. Initially, he escaped Belgrade and travelled the country under the protection of the Chetniks (noncommunist partisans). He crossed the border into Bulgaria and was soon directed by the government to leave the country. A boat across the Black Sea took the rabbi to neutral Turkey; he then made his way to British Palestine. Allied airplanes carried him across North Africa, to South America, and ultimately to New York where he served the Yugoslav government in exile as an advisor and liaison to the American Jewish community. He then served that community for another 30 years. Both Rabbi Alcalay and my grandfather Victor are buried in the same cemetery,

Grandma and Uncle Morris at a fundraising dinner for Rabbi Alcalay. (Youcha family photo)

along with Dan Elias's grandfather and just about everyone else who came from Monastir.

Maybe the letter my grandfather received in 1943 announcing the death of Jacob from natural causes followed a route similar to the rabbi's as it made its way out of Fascist-occupied Bitola?

Rabbi Alcalay's grave at the Peace and Brotherhood Society of Monastir's plot in the Beth David Cemetery, Elmont, NY. (Youcha family photo)

New York 1940s

Victor's Last Years

After World War Two started in Europe, Victor set up a business in Watertown, New York, with his brother-in-law, Rafael, making feta cheese from cow's milk. The war shut down the importation of the traditional sheep's milk feta from Bulgaria and Greece. So, there was a market. Rafael, Fortune's brother, learned cheese making from their father, Isaac, in Kir Kilisse, Turkey. Alliance documents tell us Victor studied cheesemaking at the farm school in Djédéida.

Watertown is about as far north in New York State as you can go. It's on the Saint Lawrence River. The next town north is in Canada. All the trees lean to the right because of the frigid west winter wind. My family were the first Jews many of their neighbors ever saw. Supposedly, some farmers wanted to feel their heads to see if they had horns. The family worked together at the business. My grandmother and Uncle Jack helped out for several months, while my dad stayed home in the Bronx with Aunt Beck and Aunt Annie. (Even then, Beck, at around seventeen years old, was a good cook.) Everybody pitched in. My dad remembers taking tins of cheese on the subway and delivering them throughout the city. Victor worked so hard he even missed my father's bar mitzvah in November 1940, something that seems very out of character.

After experiencing a taste of harsh winter, my grandmother swore she'd never go back again. It seems this made Victor spend more time at home in the Bronx, leaving Rafael "upstate" to practice the craft his father taught him. Unfortunately, he also practiced his drinking problem. The business didn't last long. There's a story about a big contract with a grocery store that fell through as a result of Rafael's drinking. My Uncle Morris then got Victor that job in the garment industry working as a presser. He spent the day on a machine looking at a wall, not the type of work he enjoyed doing, and a job that my dad always said killed him.

At the end, my dad remembers his father propped up in bed with lots of pillows. I feel that I can almost see it. Victor died young; he was only 56 in 1945. It was winter. He slipped on ice at work. My father accompanied him to the doctor where he was told to stop smoking. Victor replied that it was his only pleasure. He stayed in bed for a few weeks, threw an embolism, and died. At 17, my dad tried to revive him and failed. My dad remembers his mother's scream as his father's body went into the hearse. It was as if part of her soul was being torn out.

In the Beth David Cemetery, in Elmont, New York, in the section reserved for the Peace and Brotherhood Society of Monastir, the translation of Haim Victor Youcha's tombstone reads:

Here lies Our dear father
A simple and straightforward man Haim son of Reb Yaakov
Who died on 12 Shevat 5705
May his soul be [embraced] in the bond of life

My cousin (from my mom's side), Michael Shavelson, translated it from Hebrew for me and made the following comments.

> There are a few interesting things about this. *ish tam* is the first. In the Hagaddah we call the simple child "tam." In the Chumash, Yaakov is called an *ish tam*, meaning without guile. Yashar means "straight." So "ish tam v'yashar" tells me your grandfather was a straight shooter, or a no-nonsense man.
>
> The second point is that the stone says Chaim B"R Yaakov instead of Chaim ben Yaakov, which is more common, The B"R (beit resh) stands for "ben reb or rav." This is either an honorific or a declaration that your great-grandfather was a learned man.

All this lines up with everything I learned about Victor and Jacob.

My grandmother lived another 40 years after her husband died. A piece of her stayed angry with Victor for that whole time. He died right when the youngest kid, my father, was about to leave the house. Finally, they were going to have time to themselves! I remember when we buried my grandmother in the Peace and Brotherhood Society of Monastir cemetery's "new section." Once the service was over, I went with my father to Victor's grave in the "old section." We placed some rocks on his stone, and my dad said, "Well, Pop… Quiet time's over. You're going to hear it now."

The weekend that Victor died was complicated. My Aunt Beck got married two days after her father's death, on that Sunday. It was January 1945. Her fiancée, my Uncle Rubie was home on leave from the Army. The war was still going on, and there was no other option. Seventy years later, thinking about that weekend still brought tears to Beck's eyes. Growing up, I never got a complete story of what happened when my grandfather died. It was obviously a terrible event in my father's life. If he spoke about it, he only mentioned it briefly: cryptically telling stories about his mother's scream and how Uncle Morris said he was a "little boy and didn't have to go." Over the past sixty years, I built these bits of information into a story saying my father didn't go to his father's funeral. It was something I never understood, something outside of my father's character, and something he didn't want to talk about. I used to think about this as a fundamental unaddressed problem in my father's life. Then, after reading a draft of this manuscript, my ninety-five-year-old dad called me, his sixty-year-old son, and left a message saying there was something I needed to know about him.

When I called back, my dad went into detail about what happened the day of his father's death. He didn't go to the cemetery, but he did go the funeral which was held at the house. I always assumed that the religious service to mourn the end of Victor's life was graveside or at a funeral home. It never occurred to me that the memorial happened in the apartment.

My grandfather died late Thursday night. They kept his body in the house overnight, and Rabbi Isaac Cohen, a family friend, led the funeral on Friday. Serving nearby in the Army, Annie was able to make it home.

Stationed in Philadelphia with the Coast Guard, Jack didn't get home in time for either the service or the burial. After the funeral, my grandfather's coffin was carried down to the street and the waiting hearse. Here happened the only parts of this story I ever heard before. My grandmother shrieked her husband's name and thew herself on the coffin, and my Uncle Morris told my father he didn't have to go to the cemetery. My dad now tells me he objected but didn't raise a fuss with his uncle. He doesn't really know why, and neither do I. My dad was 17 and already part of the war effort. During the previous two summers, he worked away from home as a "Farm Cadet." In a few months, he enlisted in the Navy. He's never been one to back down. Maybe, as my dad speculated when I spoke to him, there just wasn't room in the car? Finding cars on short notice during wartime rationing would have been difficult. I'm also sure he didn't want to further upset his mother by making a scene. Regardless, he didn't go.

My dad, Annie, Victor, Becky, and Frieda. Circa 1937. I believe Jack took the picture on the roof of their building. (Youcha family photo)

What Kind of Past

Victor's, Frieda's, Vida's, and Morris's gravestones in Beth David Cemetery Elmont, NY. (Youcha family photos)

The loss of his father caused pain my dad's spent the last almost 80 years trying to digest. As his son, I recognized the pain, but I misplaced its origin. I thought a large part of it was guilt for "not having shown up" for his father's funeral. I was wrong about the cause, but the pain is still real. I heard it in his voice when he finally told me these stories.

Gaining a better understanding of what happened that day lets me cut away the misperceptions I generated throughout my life. It was an awful, traumatic weekend for my family, but now, finally knowing more of the story, I better understand my father's behavior. It fits in his character and isn't an outlier. This experience brings home to me the danger of incomplete stories within families getting misinterpreted by younger generations.

Map of Beth David. Monastir Peace and Brotherhood Society Block H2. (Photo by Zack Youcha)

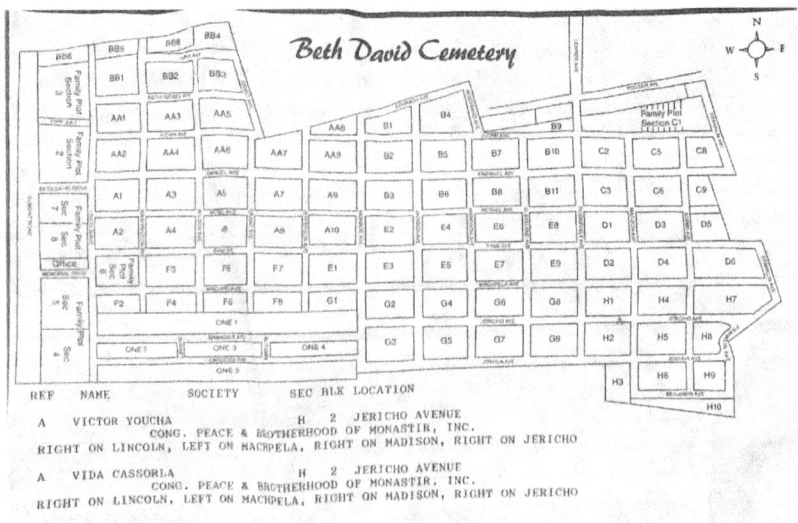

Bitola 2022

Meeting Dimitar Again

A smiling, slightly familiar face popped out of the café. It belonged to Dimitar, the archivist we met in his garden during our visit to Bitola in 2018. Meeting Dimitar was one of the first of many fortunate coincidences that facilitated this family research. This time Dimitar didn't appear by accident. In June 2022, we walked up the main pedestrian street of Bitola with Goce, the head of the local office of the national archives. He was identifying houses he knew to be Jewish and giving us an initial tour of the town. We were all on our way to dinner with him, Dimitar, their spouses, our kids, Emma and Zack, as well as their partners, Berry and Marielle.

Soon after our too-brief 2018 visit, Jessica and I decided we needed to come back to Bitola. Four years of research confirmed that belief and made us feel that our family should join us. We hoped we would be able to investigate and explore together some of the loose ends that needed to be tidied up. We might even find out something new. Rante would be our guide. We'd explore Macedonia, our interests, and see if we could "help out" in the archives.

From Rante's work with the archives, we knew resources existed that might give further information about our family and the Jewish community of Bitola. With Rante's descriptions of the facility and its basic needs, Jessica, as an archivist, knew which supplies they could use. We ended up bringing five suitcases worth of mostly acid free paper, boxes, and folders. It took all my packing skills to make sure we flew within the 23-kg limit of each piece of luggage. The supplies were greatly appreciated by the archives. Even more, we appreciated all the information and friendship they supplied us during a whirlwind two days of research, sharing, walking, eating, and drinking.

Early the next morning, after that first dinner, Goce brought his car to the hotel. We packed his tiny hatchback full of archival supplies; I could just fit into the front passenger's seat. Off we went to the archives while Rante led the rest of the group there by foot. When we arrived, we carried the supplies up to Goce's office and unpacked them on his long conference table. On the smaller table in front of his desk were arranged most of the documents he wanted to show us.

When Jessica and the rest of the crew showed up, Goce called in Dimitar and Ivana, an archival fellow especially interested in Macedonian women's history. They presented us with gifts including books and an original booklet from the 1950s which described the fate of the Jews of Bitola and commemorated their loss. A media crew then arrived and did a piece about us visiting and donating the archival materials. We later learned that we made national news!

Goce showed us Jewish photos from the collection of the Manaki brothers. Some were unexpected, like the shot of the Jewish motorcycle touring group which in the 1930s traveled from Palestine to Bitola, and beyond. (Zack wants to re-create the trip.) The building in front of which the picture was taken still exists. It's no longer a hotel, but it's first floor fittingly houses the "Manaki Bar."

Goce and Dimitar told us they just got notice they were to receive a grant from the British Library to scan all 20,000 of the Manaki photographs and related documents in their collection. These photographs capture the town and its people between the early 1900s and the 1940s. Combined with contemporaneous accounts held elsewhere—such as the Alliance archives—these photos could help tell quite a story. I also couldn't help feeling that within the Manaki collection, we might find younger versions of the Jewish faces Milton Manaki captured for the 1942 Bulgarian Police Registry.

There was one photo I wanted to find, the one that documented Rabbi Alcalay's 1914, visit to the town. I thought my great grandfather might be one of the few men wearing a fez, but in the copies I had seen, the resolution was too low to be sure. When I asked Dimitar if he knew the picture, he ushered me across the hall into his office. On his computer he had a 300-dpi scan of the glass plate negative. The better resolution showed that the person next to the Rabbi is my great grandfather Jacob. His face shows the spirit that enabled him to write the President of the Alliance four years earlier, trying to find his son. I felt I had just found out enough information to make our whole trip worthwhile.

We may have also found an image of Jacob's second wife, Bochora, from about that same time. Albert Kahn, a wealthy Jewish, French businessman, spent a large part of his fortune sending photographers around the world to take pictures of people. Kahn believed that if people could actually see other people, they wouldn't hate them and the world could be at peace. Using an early color photographic technology, Kahn's photographers circled the globe. In 1913, they stopped in Bitola/Monastir where they photographed a Jewish woman wearing a traditional headdress of gold coins. I'd seen this photo several times, but it was only after really studying the 1942 photographs that Milton Manaki took for the Bulgarian Police Registry that I realized this woman could be Bochora. In May 1913, she was 33, a reasonable age for the woman in the Kahn photograph. Being the wife of a *Mouktar*, her wearing traditional dress, and being wealthy enough to have gold coins, also makes sense. Jacob and Bochora's daughter who was killed during World War One was born around this time. Rosa would have been born the year before this photo was taken. This woman looks as if she could have just had a child or might be pregnant. The former scenario would work if Rosa and the daughter who died during the war were twins. The second scenario also works if this woman in the picture is pregnant and delivers in the next six months or so.

I ran the two photographs through photo recognition software. Using the "MyHeritage.com" software, I got an initial match, but have been unable to replicate it. Using other software, I come up with an 85% likelyhood of them being the same person. Maybe a higher resolution version of the Kahn photo and more sophisticated software will be definitive, but they sure look like the same person. It's also nice to think that we can see 1912 (or so) versions of Jacob and Bochora.

Another Photo

When we got back from our 2022 trip, I emailed my cousin Emily about the discovery of Jacob in the picture of Rabbi Alcalay's visit. She soon sent me a copy of a photo I saw many times during the research process. Taken in 1912 and set in front of the girls' school, it's the boys' school annual photo. The students stand in front of the steps, while the

Left: A close up of Jacob in a high-resolution scan of the Manaki's glass plate negative. (Courtesy of the Macedonian State Archives, Bitola) Middle: In the 1942 Bulgarian Police Registry. (Courtesy of USHMM) Right: Possibly Bochora. (Auguste Léon for Albert Kahn, Courtesy of the Albert-Kahn Departmental Museum, Department of Hauts-de-Seine, France)

1912 Alliance Boy Schools Photo with closeup of Jacob. (Courtesy of the Archives of the Alliance Israélite Universelle)

adults are above them—even in the second story windows. Emily wondered if Jacob could be in this photo, as well?

It turns out the photo comes from the Alliance Archives, and they have a fairly high resolution scan online. The photo was collected for the Alliance by Jean-Claude Kuperminc, the Archives current Director, and a behind-the-scenes supporter of Emre's research for our family. Sure enough, the higher resolution picture shows Jacob standing between two pillars on the building's porch looking prosperous, with cheeks fuller than in either of the other photographs we have of him. The picture is from 1912, the same year his daughter Roza was born, and two years after his son, Victor, arrived in New York. It's comforting to imagine that he's happy at home and really enjoying his new wife's cooking.

Searching for Roza, Finding Eliahu

When we were planning our 2022 trip, Rante told me that there was a document he found listed in the Bitola Archives which might have some information about my family. Probably written by Jacob Aroesti in the late 1950s or early 1960s as an addendum to his Yizkor book, the ledger listed Jews who originally came from Bitola but moved elsewhere. They were subsequently deported and murdered from those places during the Holocaust. When we met with Goce and his team at the archives, that register was in the stack of documents they wanted to show us.

Rante and I both thought that we might find Jacob's oldest daughter, Roza, under the listing for Greece. When he heard what we wanted to find, Goce pulled out the document and started scanning it. With his fingers running down the pages he checked every entry. No Roza. But when he started searching for Ishachs in other places he found something. Under the listing for Belgrade, in entries 7 and 8, are Eliahu Isaac Ishach and Isaac Eliahu Ishach.

Translated by Rante:

> 7. Ishah Isak Elijau [living at] str. Karadzordzeva No. 48 born 1876 in Bitola, his profession was a flour maker, he moved to Belgrade during the year 1933, where he opened a shop for

fashionable items (galanterie is the local word) that worked until the occupation. After the occupation he moved to Skopje wherefrom he was sent to the concentration camps of death together with his whole family: his wife Binuta (?) E. Ishah born 1893 in Stip, she was a housewife, his daughter Rahel E. Ishah born 1910 was a tailor, his son Rafael E. Ishah born 1916 was sales assistant, his daughter Klara E. Ishah born 1919 was a tailor and his daughter Matilda E. Ishah born 1924 in Bitola was a tailor's assistant.

8 Ishah Elijau Isak [living at] str. Karadzordzeva No. 48, born 1905 (or 3 or 7) in Bitola, from the mother Rejka (? Rejna) and father Elijau, he was a grain/flour merchant, he moved to Belgrade during 1933. He worked until the occupation and from Belgrade was taken to the camps of death, him and his wife and 3 children.

The order of the names means that Eliahu, born in 1876, was the son of a man named Isaac. The Isaac listed in row eight, born in 1906, was Eliahu's son. Eliahu was very likely Jacob's younger brother; this makes him my great great uncle. Aside from Jacob, he's the only other male Ishach from Bitola, of that age, listed in Aroesti's materials whose father was named Isaac. I believe that Aroesti got this information from the Serbian registry of the Jewish community. More relevant information might be in those documents, but until they are digitized, we won't know.

There's a saying that you die three times, once when you physically stop living, once when you're put in the ground, and once when no one remembers your name. It's sobering and sickening to document another eleven possible family members deported and murdered by the Bulgarians and Germans. It's also a bit of a comfort to know that they now will be remembered.

Ishach Occupations

Aroesti's ledger tells us that at the end of his life, Eliahu owned a shop that sold "Galanterie." The word translates as haberdasher, in the

European sense, someone who sells ribbons, needles, and "fine things." It looks like both Jacob and Eliahu worked in the same business. I wonder if they were partners? Previously, Eliahu was a grain merchant, a familiar profession for Jews in the area. In *Farewell to Salonica*, Leon Sciaky tells the story of his family in Salonica before they left in 1915. Sciaky focuses on his grandfather, a grain merchant, and gives a picture of the work and the necessary relationships with the farmers. I imagine the work would have been very similar around Bitola/Monastir. I've also run across other Ishachs who worked as grain merchants. The Youchah family tree in the University of Washington's Sephardic Studies Center lists the first ancestor as "Isaac Youchah, Grain Merchant, Had six sisters, Died at 69." Too young to be the Isaac who was Jacob's father, and

The entry in Jacob Aroesti's ledger listing Eliahu Isaac Ishach, his family, and their fate. (Courtesy of Macedonian National Archives, Bitola)

from this information, not an immediate relative, he probably connected somehow to our family.

Family tree as we know it in 2022.

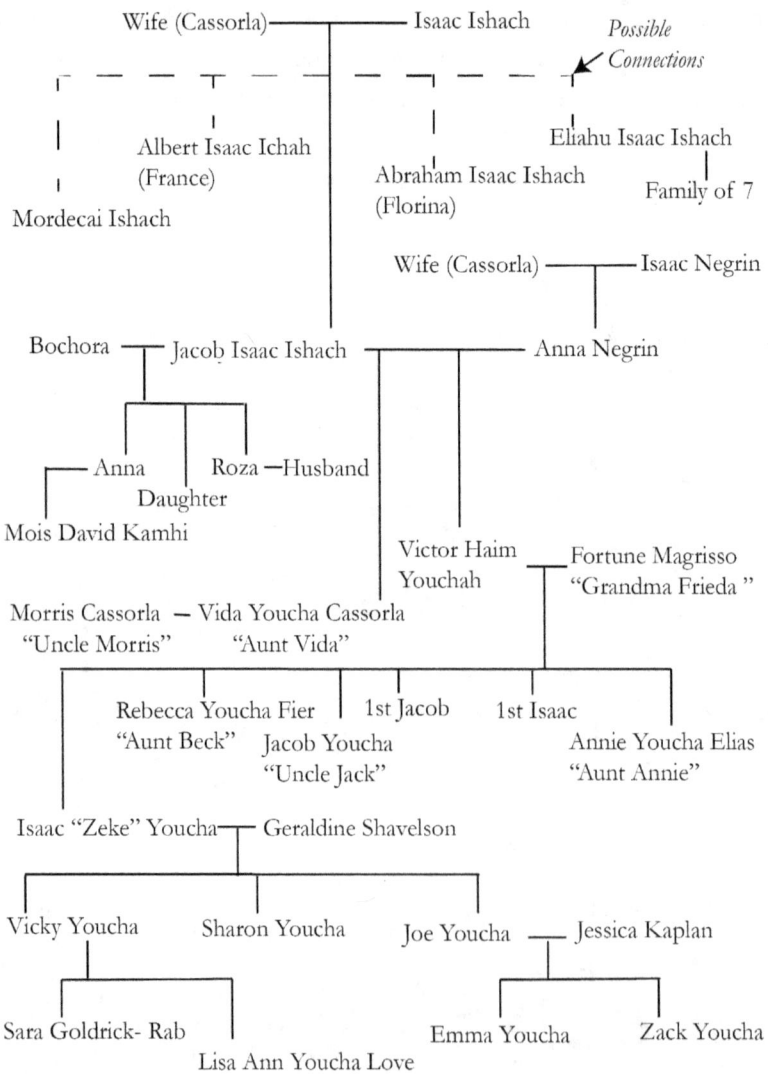

Information from Emily

When we got home from our 2022 trip, I emailed my cousin Emily and told her about finding Eliahu and his family. She sent back a copy of 2009 email correspondence between her mom and Lucie Delaporte, a member of the Ichah family in France. It seems possible that Abraham Albert Ichah, Lucie's great grandfather born in Monastir on October 13th, 1898, was Jacob's nephew. Abraham's father's name was "Albert Isaak Ichah." His father's name had also been Isaac. The timing works out well for Albert to be Jacob's brother. My dad always hopefully speculated that he might have relatives in France. Maybe he does?

Jacob possibly had a third brother. Using the results of DNA testing, Cousin Emily connected with Ethan Russo, a Monastirli living near Seattle. Ethan's ancestor, Mordecai Ishach was either Jacob's brother or first cousin.

Possible pieces of Jacob's family are starting to fill in. Eliahu from Belgrade, Abraham from Florina, Albert from France, and Mordecai through his great great grandson, Ethan Russo, in Seattle. It's all part of a continuing story that goes back centuries.

The Scrolls

I found out about the scrolls because of Steven Sage. One of the main reasons he went to Bitola was to inspect the old documents. When Steven got to the archives, Goce and his team knew the scrolls were Jewish, but they didn't know what type of scroll they were or what texts they contained. Steven freely admits that he is no "heder boy"—someone who grew up going to traditional Jewish religious schools. Yet, through some basic reading of the Hebrew, he figured out that in the longer scroll the word הרטפה (*haftarah*) appears frequently. Therefore, it makes sense that the scroll was a *haftarah*, a selection from the Prophets in the Bible. Using Google search, Steven determined that the shorter fragments were from the Deuteronomy, specifically 7.12 to 14.2. So, they were part of a Torah.

Steven confirmed his findings with Professor Gershon Greenberg at American University. It was a *haftarah*, and they were Torah fragments.

Describing the situation as he read the scrolls, Steven said,

It was a very moving moment for me, my thumb on one end of a scroll fragment that a scribe had hand copied about six or seven hundred years ago, probably somewhere in Spain or Portugal, before the expulsions of 1492–1497. These scrolls had been treasured, brought to Monastir long ago, and had been read and studied in the synagogue by generations of rabbis and genuine heder boys all the way down to the year 1943. The partial scroll is a tangible remnant that belonged to a vanished, martyred community.

Steven next needed to figure out where the scrolls came from, were they Sephardic? Written using a reed, rather than a quill, which was the standard for Ashkenazi texts, the scrolls conformed to the Sephardi style. Calligraphic style corroborated the 13th–15th century CE dating. To be more exact about the scrolls' origins, Steven thinks they need to be analyzed by a specialized scholar. The best are in Paris and Israel.

On our first morning in the Bitolan Archives, Goce brought out the scrolls. They are prized possessions. We were only the fifth group to see them. My feelings were much as Steven's. I was a bit awed by touching once sacred scrolls, carried from Spain over 500 years ago. Even more powerful for me were my kids' reaction to the scrolls. Both Emma and Zack were obviously very moved, and very engaged in examining these pieces of our past.

As Steven described, the *haftarah* scroll has drawings on its back. Zack and Emma figured out these kid's scribbles include one that looks like a rabbi. These texts are usually only written with consonants, but Emma and Zack saw there were passages with vowels added in a different ink— as if someone were learning to read the passage out loud. All this points to the scroll being used as a teaching tool, possibly in the Talmud Torah.

Seeing if we could help the Bitolan Archives preserve these pieces of our heritage seemed logical. When Steven saw them, he questioned how the scrolls were made and what materials were used—information key to helping develop a conservation and storage plan. Steven wasn't sure if some of the parchment was backed onto thick paper. Nor was he sure the scrolls were stored in acid free boxes.

There are advantages when you bring a traditional bookbinder with you. Emma figured out that the scrolls are likely written on goatskin parchment, as would be traditional. This will help in developing the scroll's preservation plan. Emma also plans to make acid free boxes to better store the scrolls.

The scrolls came to the archives in 1954. There are no detailed records about the acquisition. Perhaps Jacob Aroesti saved them? We don't know. I remember hearing, likely from Goce, a rumor that the scrolls were dug up. The Torah fragments not only look very old, they look as if they could have been burnt. We know that in the 1830s, '60s, and '90s, fires damaged the Jewish neighborhoods and synagogues. Under Jewish law a damaged Torah or sacred text that can't be repaired is placed in a *Genizah*—a room or space where it can't be destroyed. Many times, the contents of a *Genizah* are then buried in a cemetery, just like a person. It's possible the community buried these damaged scrolls in the cemetery? Perhaps they were buried in the yard of the old synagogue, Kal Aragon, and dug up when that area was redeveloped for the hospital and roundabout?

Dimitar, Zack, Emma, Berry, and Marielle examine the Haftarah scroll. (Joe Youcha photo)

Zack seems fascinated by the possibility of more documents being buried at the synagogue site. The 1943 *Jerusalem Post* article detailing Rabbi Alcalay's escape says that sacred objects throughout Yugoslavia were buried by congregations as soon as the Germans invaded the country. So, Zack's interest is justified. Perhaps he'll find a way to determine if there are more objects buried at the synagogue site. It could well be a lifetime project.

Buildings and Neighborhoods in Bitola

Since figuring out that Jacob really was an Ottoman *Mouktar*, I'd tried to discover what that meant in his life. What were his responsibilities? Who did he serve? Was he responsible for the whole Jewish community, or was it just a Jewish neighborhood?

In the Alliance director's report, which relays one of Jacob's letters to Paris, the director says that Jacob was *Mouktar* of the Ali Taouch neighborhood. By connecting a few dots, Rante and I figured out the rough boundaries of this neighborhood. The first clue came from Emre. In his research of the Alliance documents, he found that the girls' school was located on Ali Taouch Street.

The building still exists. It's owned by the Macedonian Jewish community. We saw it on the first evening of our 2022 to trip to Bitola. The street is now called Roosevelt. It's on the south side of the Dragor river, across the river from the old Jewish neighborhood, where Jacob is listed as living in the 1930s Serbian Jewish community register and the 1942 Bulgarian police registry. His living in the neighborhood he supervised during Ottoman rule would make sense. If he had lived there in 1909, what made him move back across the river?

Even after years of hardship and neglect, the houses in the neighborhood are still nice, many with balconies and courtyards. Using Steven Sage's technique of looking for *mezzuzot* holes on door frames, we determined that many of these houses were Jewish at one time.

It's easy to imagine Jacob living in this neighborhood when he was *Mouktar* under the Turks and doing well as a *seraph* (moneychanger). Then, after the Balkan Wars took his position and the city was destroyed during the First World War, Jacob could have moved to less expensive housing in "La Kalaze," the old Jewish neighborhood, where he's listed in both later registries. The fire of 1897 likely forced Jacob to accept free school uniforms for Victor from the Alliance. Did the destruction of a house in the old Jewish neighborhood make Jacob and his family move to a new house across the river? Ottoman census records available in Istanbul may tell us if Jacob ever lived in the Ali Taouch neighborhood, what the Jews called "La Malle." Emre tried to help me figure it out, but the records are in Ottoman Turkish, a dead language written in a modified Arabic script. That's another research project to pursue.

Regardless, we know the rough outlines of the neighborhood. It contained the Alliance schools, which might explain Jacob's influence with the schools' directors, how he was able to get Victor to Tunisia and then able to have the school's directors relay his letters to the president of the Alliance in Paris.

Rante was better able to define the boundaries of the neighborhood after a conversation with Alexander Sterjovski, a local historian now researching historic Bitolan neighborhoods. Goce, the archives director, asked Alexander to come and meet us on our first day in Bitola. He came

Map of La Malle, or Ali Taouch neoghborhood, 2022. (Courtesy of Bojan Rantasa)

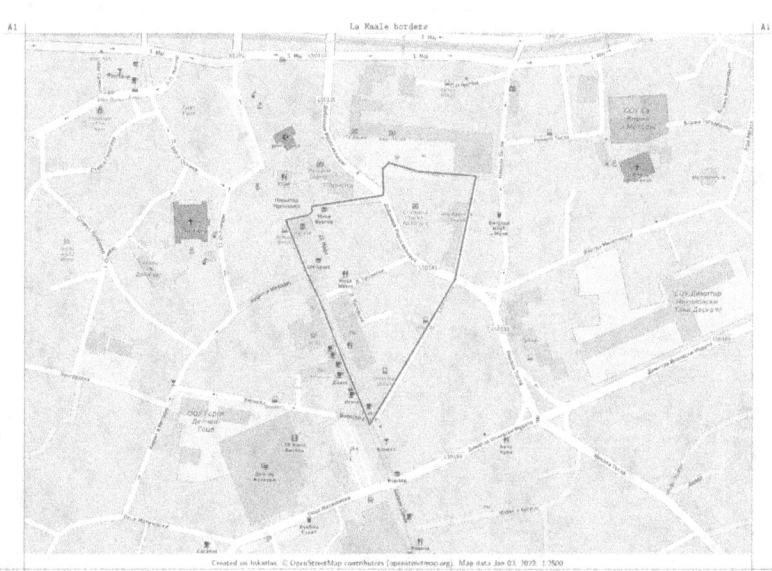

to the archives with a friend, but he was a little distant, polite but not really engaging. Once he figured out that he, Zack, Marielle, and Jessica all spoke Russian, the reserve came down. When Rante showed him the map on his phone, he confirmed that was the Ali Taouch neighborhood. It was bounded by Roosevelt Street and Shirok Sokak—the major pedestrian street. However, we have to wait for all the details until he publishes his next book. I think it will be his sixteenth. I wish I thought to ask the identity of Ali Taouch. I read he was an Ottoman hero, but I don't know any details. I guess I will have to wait for Alexander's book.

While everyone talked about streets changing their names over time, I asked Dimitar about the book he used in 2018 to locate Bulgarian Lozengrad Street. Could I see it? He looked at me a little quizzically and said that it wasn't there. The book wasn't part of the archives. It was his personally, once owned by his grandfather, a mailman. So, during that first coincidence in Dimitar's garden, we really fulfilled Rante's wish and "found an old postman"—or at least his grandson.

Bitola's Talmud Torah 2022. (Joe Youcha photo)

The Talmud Torah

I don't want to be sentimental about "walking the streets my ancestors walked," but so much Jewish influence remains in Bitola—whether it's the *mezzuzot* holes on so many doorways or the Tuesday and Friday market days that still avoid the Jewish Sabbath. Probably the most remarkable building we saw was the old Talmud Torah.

Goce told us he was taking us somewhere special. We were in the old bazaar, in front of a liquor store. After ducking in the store's small dark entrance and making a quick left, we went out the back of the store into a courtyard. Before us was a three-story building. It was being fixed up by the liquor store owner but still had a long way to go. It was Monastir's Talmud Torah, or traditional Hebrew school.

The Jewish community built, maintained, and supported the building whose story reflects the complicated, painful history of the town. Many of the tiles are marked with the Alitani factory's imprint, probably donations from that wealthy Jewish family in Salonica. According to the current owner of the Talmud Torah building, who also owns the liquor store, after the deportation and murder of the Jews in 1943, the building housed war refugees, later sheltered people displaced by the nearby Greek Civil War, and then was used for manufacturing and storage. Recently, the owner is restoring the building in hopes it becomes a museum. He's working without help from the local or Jewish communities. To an outsider, it doesn't make sense, but, as Rante says, "It's the Balkans…"

I read about the Talmud Torah in the Alliance records. The schools complemented and supported one another. It seems almost all the younger boys went first to the Talmud Torah. When they were about eight or nine, the better students transferred over to the Alliance boy's school. If anything didn't go well there they were sent back to the Talmud Torah. The Alliance director's reports repeatedly document this back-and-forth of students.

The Alliance also financially supported and supervised the Talmud Torah—although it wasn't the only means of financial support for the religious school. The Jewish religious court (Bet Din) levied fines on those guilty of breaking Jewish law. One of the beneficiaries of those monies was the free meal fund at the Talmud Torah. At different times, several of the rabbis sitting on the religious court were relatives of Dan Elias (the musician.)

Almost certainly, my grandfather, and possibly his father, went to school here. So did the male ancestors of all the Monastirlis I've met during this research. Without a surviving synagogue in Bitola, this building ties us together. It's also possible that the long *haftarah* scroll in the archive came from here, and that the rabbi depicted in the kid's cartoon on the scroll's back once taught mischievous students here.

The Train Station

At the end of our 2022 stay in Bitola, our last stop was the train station. It hasn't changed much from the 1914 picture where Jacob stood with the rest of the male leadership of newly renamed Bitola and welcomed Rabbi Alcalay. I hopped out of the van, took some pictures, and stood approximately where my great grandfather stood in that photo. The station certainly played a role in my family's life. Young Victor probably left from there to start his journey to the Alliance farm school in Tunisia. Lastly, this station was the initial destination of all the Jews being deported from Bitola on March 11, 1943. They walked a little over a mile from their homes to be loaded into rail cars and sent to Skopje. This building

Bitola's Train Station 2022. (Joe Youcha photo)

witnessed my family's hope, acknowledgment of change, and horror. Despite what it saw, today it still looks the same as it did in 1914.

Train station are places where journeys start, end, and continue, an apt metaphor for my family's story. While doing this research, I thought a lot about what gets carried forward to future generations, what gets taught—especially to young people—about life's beauty, love, and horror. I realized our family journey continues with the current generations engaged and actively looking to reconnect and continue our heritage, as well as bringing the lessons to others who might be able to use them. I no longer see my father's family as black and white caricatures. They are much more nuanced. I feel I've gotten to know them a bit—especially my great grandfather Jacob. His great great grandchildren are interested in him, his life, and his town. His grandson has changed his view of him. We rediscovered and will remember his second family. Maybe we are finding his brothers and their families. We will remember them, as well.

My children are acting on what they've learned and experienced. Emma wants to go back to Bitola and help look for materials in Ladino and preserve objects in the archives. Zack is working with Dan Elias to remaster his family's recordings and bring together a group of musicians in New York who are connected to Bitola. They'll then bring the music back to Macedonia and help continue building bridges between the cultures.

As I wrote these stories down, I thought a lot about my college professor, Yosef Yerushalmi and reread his book about history and memory. In it, he says that how we remember, what we choose to remember, and what we reclaim are purposeful choices. I realized that if I'd have listened to him carefully forty years ago, Professor Yerushalmi would have told me something I've learned over the last four years: "The choice for Jews as for non-Jews is not whether or not to have a past, but rather—what kind of past shall one have."

Afterword: Our Name

In Macedonia

Before we went on our 2018 trip, one of the big questions that hung over my cousins Linda and Emily's family research was figuring out our last name in Macedonia. There are no "Youcha's" listed on the German deportation documents.

My dad always felt that our last name came from the Hebrew of Joshua, "Yoshua." At a party one night, the editor of *Coronet Magazine*, where my mother worked in the late 1940s and early 1950s, said this might be true. Frits Bamberger was a German Jewish scholar who commanded respect and to whom my mom was devoted. Mr. Bamberger thought our name could be from the Romaniotes—Greek Jews who lived in the area before the Sephardim settled there. It's a romantic idea, but my cousins' research poked too many holes in it.

One of the books the curator at the Holocaust Museum in Skopje gave me in 2018 resolved the issue. In the preface to Schlomo Alboher's *The Jews of Monastir*, Dr. Nissim Yosha says that in Bitola his name, which is roughly the same as ours, was Ishach. Period. End of sentence.

Also interesting was a theory of where the name could come from. In his chapter about Monastir's Jewish names, Alboher says the name comes from Isaac. Dr. Yosha says this is possible, but that it could also be a corruption of the name Ischer. This is how the Jews pronounced the name of the city now called Hijar in the Spanish province, Aragon. And, the name of Ishach was only used by Jews originating in Monastir, many of whom came from Aragon.

In Spain

After the rest of us flew home from our 2022 trip to Macedonia, Zack and Marielle continued to Greece, Spain, and Portugal. They unsuccessfully searched for Jacob's daughter Roza in the archives of the Jewish community in Thessaloniki. In Spain they went to Aragon, to Zaragoza, and for a day to Hijar.

Zack and Marielle took the bus from Zaragoza to Hijar, where they met Lucia Aguilar, a professor at the University of Barcelona in medieval history. Their path to Lucia started when Jessica found an article mentioning Lucia's work restoring Hijar's synagogue and the surrounding old Jewish neighborhood. Zack got in touch and found out that Lucia would be visiting her parents the weekend when he would be there.

Lucia comes from an old Hijar family and studies pre-Inquisition Jewish history. From her research she realized that her family were probably "conversos," fifteenth-century Jewish converts whose families still bear remnants of Judaism as superstitions. Many local Hijar families share Sephardic last names. They also retain customs. Twisted candles are lit in special candle stick holders on Saturday evenings. This is a remnant of lighting *havdallah* candles to signify the end of the Jewish sabbath. Many traditions that became Spanish are actually thinly veiled Jewish ones. And it's the same the other way around. Through her research, Lucia realized she grew up with those types of superstitions. The discovery led her to become a Jew.

Zack FaceTimed me from inside the synagogue of Hijar showing me the location of the Torah ark that once stored sacred scrolls, such as the fragments we saw in the Bitolan Archives. He showed me the excavation of the raised platform, the *bimah*, from which the Torah had been read. And, he pointed out exposed Hebrew script on the walls. Zack and Marielle brought Lucia a bottle of wine to say thank you. Lucia asked if Zack wanted to be the first Jew from Hijar in 500 years to say Kaddish and the Shema. Zack said he's not a big spiritual guy, but that the way he felt being there, saying the prayers felt like "spiritual clarity."

My son also said that he found our last name literally "written in stone." In the 1980s, the city of Hijar redid the streets leading out of the Jewish quarter. Mosaics of the Star of David are next to those of the city

Zack and Lucia saying Kaddish in front of recess for the Torah ark. (Marielle Czerniecki photo)

shield showing the name of the town as spelled in its original Castilian, Ishahr. Apparently, the last "r" is soft. It's our last name.

Zack told me that Hijar is called the city of percussion. The music starts on the Shabbat before Easter. Old families march around town and end up with a communal meal in the old Jewish quarter. They're having Passover without knowing it. Lucia did a seminar on the Jewish community for the people of Hijar. They asked her two questions. "How come Jews are so smart?" And, "Can I touch you? I didn't know Jews existed."

Lucia got very emotional meeting Zack. She told him that the Hebrew of our last name is very similar to the only Jewish name she can trace back to Hijar using primary documents. It's a letter from a rabbi who went to Safed in Palestine. He signed his name de Ishar. Lucia has been in touch with his descendants who still live in Israel and wants to connect Zack to his distant cousins.

I asked Zack to see if people looked like us there. I was thinking about Joe Elias's story about going to Cassorla in Spain and feeling like

Left: Picture of the Hijar's Castilian Seal. Right: Hebrew writing on Hijar synagogue wall. (Zack Youcha photo)

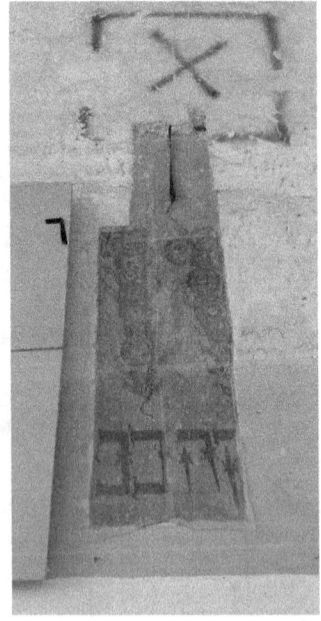

everybody looked like his family. It seems that most of the people in Hijar look like most Youchas, short and broad.

The Jewish neighborhood of Hijar is privately owned, but problematically, the synagogue belongs to no one. After the Inquisition, the synagogue become a Franciscan Chapel. Until the ceiling collapsed recently, it was used once a year to celebrate St. Andrew. In her efforts to fix the building, Lucia reached out to the bishop who said that the Catholic Church never had a deed to the property. After the expulsion of the Jews, the church just took it. There was no document. Now, the building is in limbo. Lucia secured a European Union grant which paid for a new roof and foundation repair. In the repair process, they were also able to do some minor excavations, discovering the Torah Ark right behind the

Page with Jewish printer's seal. (Zack Youcha photo)

Zack standing in arch of the women's entrance to the Kal. (Marielle Czerniecki photo)

shrine of St. Anthony and a painting of a menorah under a portrait of Jesus, as well as the Hebrew script. Zack sent a picture of him standing under the arch of the women's entrance to the synagogue.

Lucia gets her research information about the Jewish community of the 1490s from Inquisition documents, mostly about people who converted and the trials against fake converts. There are reports about catching a group of "false converts" when they went to the synagogue courtyard and listened to the sacred music on Shabbat. Lucia and her friends now own the building that contains this courtyard.

Lucia told Zack about the town's history of Jewish printing. The Hebrew typeface developed in Hijar was the best in all of Spain. Before 1492, the Jewish print shop served as a safe house for Jews fleeing the Inquisition from other regions. It was the second oldest Jewish print shop in Spain. After the 1492 expulsions, the printer fled Hijar with his type and press to Lisbon, then to North Africa, and then to Greece and Turkey. The typeface still exists. Samples of the printing show Hebrew type with notes printed in Rashi, the Hebrew font of Sephardic Jews. The print house was the first ever to have a printing seal. It's a lion with a shield.

The experiences in Macedonia and Spain were eye-opening for Zack. People in Bitola miss our culture and want to understand it. Obviously, a piece of Spain feels the same. Lucia told Zack, "I have the object. You [Jewish families from Aragon] have the memories."

As a father, it's amazing that Zack went to Hijar, made the connection with the historian to get into the synagogue, and said the prayers. Possibly figuring out where our last name comes from in Spain is tremendous, but what's really wonderful is that he was so obviously moved. It's going to be very interesting to see where he takes this, or where this takes him. By "going home," he acted on an idea our family pondered for 500 years.

Acknowledgments

Putting this story together involved an exceptional set of coincidences which occurred as the result of meeting remarkable people. Almost all these people are now friends—one of the best things about this project. I'm sure I'm leaving some people out. For that, I apologize. The fault is mine, but their help is deeply appreciated.

Research in Macedonia depended upon our friend Bojan Rantasa, "Rante." Rante performed a lot of work on his own and connected us to many people, particularly those at the State Archives of the Republic of Northern Macedonia—Bitola Department: Goce Stojanovski, Dimitar Gjorgievski, and Ivana Hadjievska. Goran Sadikarijo, the director of the Holocaust Memorial Center for Jews of Macedonia and his staff also supported all our work and answered many questions. Joseph Benatov our Balkan Sephardic tour guide in 2018 always graciously provided innumerable leads, contacts, translations, and context.

The archives of the Alliance Israelite Universelle in Paris provided the greatest source of documents relating to my grandfather, Victor, and his father, Jacob. The director, Jean-Claude Kuperminc pointed us in the right direction and made his staff available to find and scan innumerable documents. Jean-Claude also connected us to Emre Yarvuz, who discovered my grandfather in the documents and traced his trail from Monastir, Djédéida, to Canada. The discovery of those documents is a gift for which my family will always be grateful. Thanks also go to Elizabeth Vernon at Harvard University's Library for her help navigating their copies of the Alliance documents.

Fellow Monastirlis Mark Cohen and his book, *Last Century of a Sephardic Community*, offer resources upon which any future research of Monastir will stand. Steven Sage from the United State Holocaust Memorial

Museum is a walking encyclopedia, one of whose volumes fortunately involves the fate of the Bitolan Jews during the Holocaust. And, Dr. Emil Kerenji, an Applied Research Scholar and family friend, connected us to resources at the Museum and to Steven.

My French was good enough for me to read through the Alliance documents, but for important passages, I relied on friends of my son Zack. Fred Gagliolo and Guillaume Rebeyrol both translated many letters and cleared up questions my forty-year-old French couldn't puzzle out. I also owe my cousin, Michael Shavelson, for the translation and interpretation of the Hebrew on my grandfather's tombstone. Janice Rosen, Archives Director at the Canadian Jewish Archives, went well out of her way to find correspondence concerning my grandfather's fate in western Canada.

Since this is a family story, much of it depends on the stories my family told me by my father, Isaac Zeke Youcha, his sister, my Aunt Beck, Rebecca Youcha Fier, and Aunt Beck's daughter, Linda Fier Hirsch.

As I said in the text, I'm not the first to do family research. My cousins, Linda and Emily Youcha, uncovered way more than I, and shared unstintingly.

The musical aspect of this story provided an unexpected pleasure. Meeting and learning from Ara Dinkjian, Dan Elias, and through his recordings Joe Elias continues to teach me music. David Rapkievian, Chris Pantzelos, Tasos Theodorakis, and John Vergara all enabled me to build my oud.

Writing is a craft, just like boat building or lutherie. Writing can't happen without critical readers. For that, I thank my niece Lisa Ann Youcha Love, Carol Crawford, my teacher at the John C. Campbell Folk School, as well as my children Emma and Zack.

Finally, without my wife, Jessica, who served as researcher, reader, and editor, as well as being the person who gives me the love and support I need to lead my life, none of this would have been possible.

Resource Pages

Southern Balkan Jewish History—In a Nutshell
- Monastir
  - Mark Cohen's *The Last Century of a Sephardic Community*. A terrific book with excellent notes and bibliography.
- Salonica
  - Devin Naar, *Jewish Salonica*. A comprehensive view of Jewish history in Salonica.
  - *Farewell to Salonica: Portrait of an Era*, Leon Sciaky. Lovely memoir.

Bitola, North Macedonia, June 2018
- The Holocaust Memorial Center for Jews of Macedonia
  - http://www.holocaustfund.org/
- *The Jews of Monastir* by Shlomo Alboher
  - A Jew born in Bitola who immigrated to Palestine before World War Two, Alboher wrote a book that combines history with a memorial to the destroyed community.

New York Arlington, Virginia 2019
- Mark Cohen's book is a great source that helps put the information in context.
- Devin Naar's article on the Jewish White Supremacy Problem
  - https://jewishcurrents.org/our-white-supremacy-problem/
- Alliance Bulletins: The National Library of Israel has online copies of these documents. They are in French.
  - http://www.jpress.nli.org.il/Olive/APA/NLI/?action=tab&tab=browse&pub=bul&_ga=2.28502972.1801878358.1534554758-763885550.1534554758#panel=document

- ○ United States Holocaust Museum and Memorial Photo Archive, Photos of Jews deported from Bitola. Go to the photo archives and search for "Bitola."
    - https://www.ushmm.org/search/results/?q=bitola
- Yad Vashem web exhibit about the Jews of Monastir/Bitola
    - ○ https://www.yadvashem.org/yv/en/exhibitions/communities/monastir/index.asp
- Link to Jacob Aroesti's Yizkor book in the New York Public Library Digital Collections
    - ○ https://digitalcollections.nypl.org/items/7bba8840-9950-0134-210d-00505686a51c/book#page/3/mode/2up

Manaki Brothers
- https://en.wikipedia.org/wiki/Yanaki_and_Milton_Manaki
- *Last album: Keeper of Memories of the Jewish Religious Community*, Alexander Manojlovski
    - ○ Rare book published in Macedonia about the Jewish photographs of the Manakis. Only 100 copies were printed. Rante got me one.
- *Braka Manaki = Manaki Kardeşler : Balkanların ilk sinematografları = Manaki Brothers : first cinematographers in the Balkans*
    - ○ Manaki Films DVD of conserved films with excellent booklet. Some of the films are also on YouTube.

Music, Building Musical Instruments, and the Oud
- Luthiers
    - ○ David Rapkievian https://fineviolinsbydavid.com/
    - ○ Tasos Theodorakis https://xilofonia.gr/
    - ○ Chris Pantzelos, Spartan Instruments: http://www.spartaninstruments.com/
    - ○ John Vergara Lord of the Strings: https://www.johnvergaramusic.com/
- Musicians
    - ○ Ara Dinkjian https://www.aradinkjian.com/
    - ○ Charbel Rouhana https://charbelrouhana.org/
    - ○ Flory Jagoda: https://en.wikipedia.org/wiki/Flory_Jagoda

- ○ The Elias Ladino Ensemble. Here's a 1997 performance: https://www.youtube.com/watch?v=GEXs_RNK4Lg
- Archival Resources
  - ○ Link to Mandolin Orchestra Picture: USHMM: https://collections.ushmm.org/search/catalog/pa1119053
  - ○ ILGWU Archive, Cornell University: https://ilgwu.ilr.cornell.edu/archives/
  - ○ Sephardic Brotherhood of America: https://www.sephardicbrotherhood.com/
  - ○ Alliance Israelite Universelle Archives: https://www.aiu.org/en/archives-0
    - Alliance Bulletins: http://www.jpress.nli.org.il/Olive/APA/NLI/?action=tab&tab=browse&pub=bul&_ga=2.73459218.1801878358.1534554758-763885550.1534554758#panel=document
  - ○ *Cinquante ans d'histoire L'Alliance Israelite (50 Years...)*, Narcisse Leven
    - https://gallica.bnf.fr/ark:/12148/bpt6k2069487/f329.item

Monastir, Djédéida, and Canada 1903–1910

- AIU Digital Exhibit on Jews of Monastir
  - ○ https://www.bibliotheque-numerique-aiu.org/en/exhibitions-us/exhibitions/67-the-jews-of-monastir-bitola
- Accessing AIU documents
  - ○ I accessed digitized AIU documents through Harvard's HOLLIS library. Hopefully, everything will soon be available through the AIU archives. The documents of the Former Yugoslavia are currently being digitized. (2022) Here are the basic steps, courtesy of Emily Youcha.
  - ○ **Step 1: Use the Alliance Archives to find your file numbers.**
    - Go to the website http://www.archives-aiu.org/aiu/index.htm.
    - Search for the place or person of interest.
    - Get the file name for the search results, such as: "Turquie VIII E 157."

- Step 2. Go to the Harvard Hollis library to download the PDF files. https://hollis.harvard.edu/ primo-explore/ search?vid=HVD2& lang=en_US&sortby=rank.
  - Search for the desired file name: **Alliance Israelite Universelle archives: Turkey: File(s) VIII E**
  - Remember you will have to search in English, so change Turquie to Turkey.
- Emre Yarvuz's initial list of AIU documents pertaining to Victor. There are more in the Tunisia files.
  - Yougoslavie, I E, Ecoles, Monastir
    - Ecoles 1902–1904, Arié David, directeur, No: 4
    - 28 July 1903
      - Two application sheets for Djédéida. Haim Youcha et Elie Graciani could probably be mentioned here.
    - 4 Septembre 1903
      - Scheduled departure of the 6 students in the direction of Tunisia and Palestine.
    - 22 Mai 1904
      - 4 students give full satisfaction to their directors.
    - 27 Juin 1904
      - Mr. Antebi and Mr. Avigdor appreciate the Monastriotes students.
  - Ecoles 1905–1906, Arié David, directeur, No: 5
    - 30 Mars 1905
      - 40 francs sent for 4 students from Monastır to Djéidéida. They would be the following students: Haim Youcha, Elie Graciani, Samuel Cavo, Elie Massoth.
    - 2 Juillet 1905
      - The principals in Mikveh and in Tunisia are satisfied with the Monastriote students. Mr. Arié is optimistic that Monastir will become a fertile field for agriculture and that the Jews are pioneers, especially those in agricultural schools.

- 14 Aout 1905
  - Two other students from Monastir are admitted to Djédéida: Samuel Farasez and Moise Israel.
- The students shown in the exhibition photo would probably be these two students in the presence of Victor Chickly.
- 18/20 April 1906
  - Eliezer Arié is in Djéidéida for a school trip. He is the son of David Arié, the director of schools in Monastir.
- Schools 1907–1908, Arié David, director, No: 6
  - 6 September 1908
    - Youcha, after 5 years in Djéidéida, sent to Canada.
  - Jacob Youchah is Mouhtar from the Ali Tchaouch district and the father of Haim.
- Tunisia V E 001p—Mr. Avigdor—Djédéida.
  - May 16, 1906: Report on the settlement movement in Canada
- MOS-EN 16.21: Statistics of students in Djéidéida
- MOS-EN 16-23-0008: Lists of promotions in Djédéida
- France X F 18.05, 1895–1913: Annual reports of directors in Monastir
  - List of graduates 1902–1903. Haim Youcha studied for 4 years at the Monastir School.

- AIU Tunisian Documents Found in Microfilm Rolls with my notes and page references for these pdf files
  - Tunisia II hijk
    - P 40 (and around). Letters describing necessity of work after graduation
      - Keeping up current students' hope
      - Setting up Sharecropping
      - Also, don't send students who can't take the heat. Locals are the first choice. Those from Europe and the Balkans are the last choice.
    - P 720. Description of courses at school
    - P 729. Article about the school
    - P 878. Map of area
    - P 902. Enrolling class of 1903–4

- P 916. Information about class of 1905–6
- PP 928–9. Letter about the new admissions. Sums up his worry about new arrivals from Balkans not being able to handle the weather.
- P 942. Map
- PP 1006–7. Possible mention of Turc apprentices arriving in September
- PP 1008–12. Recommendations for reform: Only serve north African students and demographics of higher grades. Wants to shorten program, make it less academic—less French, no advanced math—and focus on North African students.
- PP 1084–5. More about the failures of Turkish and Bulgarian students
- PP 1085–1095. Report on subjects taught by year and instructors
- PP 1102–3. Annual report segment about Bulgarian and Turkish students—maybe the arrival of students
- P 1115. Note on back/reply "eleves Youcha et…" Maybe…
- He writes: "les éleves déja sortis" and "nos anciens éleves Jouda…"
- PP 1157–?. Report on the history and physical condition as well as purpose of the school for a visit by the resident general Stephan Pinchon (27th Septembre 1901–29 Decembre 1906). Pinchon visited the Farm School in 1903. Source: Archives israélites de France, Vol. 64 Nu: 7, 19).

○ Tunisia II k
- P 16–21. Bulgarian kids are troublemakers, "anarchists in the field." Really a screed.
- PP 23–26. The new students write home saying they want to go home. The promises made by the Alliance aren't met by the reality of the farm school.
- P 39. Maybe mentions Graziani (fellow student from Monastir)

- PP 46–48. More about the kids wanting to go home and the false expectations given the parents and family
- P 49. Letter from a father asking for his son to be returned from the school because he only has two professors, etc…
- PP 62–66. Letter from Leon Israel (recent student in Algeria?) to third year students. A letter for an uprising! The story of the mutiny is in between with letters of apology from the kids.
- P 116. List of Professors
- P 213. B. Boccara readmitted to school. He eventually went with my Grandfather to Canada.
- P 217. Letter from Boccara's father, Reuben. They were from Tunis.
- P 296. 1903–04 admissions by country. Two from Turkey. Must be the ones from Monastir. Avigdor still wants to suspend the admission of Turks and Bulgarians to the farm school.
- P 317. "Magrisso" shows up. (My Grandmother's name.)

○ Tunisia II E pqr
- P 9. Gracian from the Dardanelles (?) goes to Egypt. Is this the same student from Monastir who went to the school with my Grandfather? When Avigdor refers to "Monastir," I believe he is talking about the town in Tunisia.
- P 109. The changes that have been made in the last few years
- P 106. English Class. The Central Committee had already decided to send students from Djédéida to Canada by October 15th, 1906. They were to be taught English one hour a day outside of class. Mr. Cohen, the proposed teacher, needed to get an extra allowance for teaching the class.
- P 132. Avigador wants to build a café/restaurant at the Djédéida train station. It would be run by an honorable local family. (Wonder if my grandfather was involved?)
- P 137. They are building two new farms for the "young colonists" and name them the Leven Farms.
- P 278. Avigdor gives a history of the school

- P 433. June 1906 letter from Avigdor to Cazes about students going to Canada
- P 436. June 20, 1906, letter from Cazes to Avigdor about students going to Canada
- PP 1182–3. 2/11/07 Eleve Youchah asks to go to Canada in place of Enrique Guido
- P 1187. 2/6/07 Initial letter with list of original students going to Canada with descriptions
- Tunisia II E 1 lmno
  - P 58. Letter from Avigdor talking about Turkish students working in Bulgaria. June 1904.
  - PP 59–60. Letter from students. Including Mitrani.
  - P 61. Letter from Avigdor on same subject
  - P 88. It looks like Avigdor's wife died and the Portuguese community in Tunis paid for the burial.
  - P 137. Looks like the original idea for establishing a Jewish agricultural village and naming it after Leven.
  - P 142. Letter about sending students to Dobrudja, "Colons Russes." Question about foreign Jews owning land.
  - P 156. Letter about Bulgarian colony and Turks not being able to own land
  - P 170. Telegram Mme Avigdor died last night 15 May 1904
  - P 202. Map of land that might be bought
  - PP 211–30. Program of studies for the school in 1904
  - P 272. Annual report 02–03; this was a rough year. Avigdor had to clean house of tough students.
  - P 332. Letter from student who tried to go to Argentina but was turned away because they were only taking applicants from their home countries. Didn't want to go to Cyprus. Wants to stay in Tunisia. December 1903.
  - P 345. Sending a student, Bouraglo, to Brazil
  - P 353. Turkish and Bulagarian students need to learn Arabic if they are going to be sent to Egypt. The instruction isn't necessary for Algerian and Tunisian students because they'll

be working in their home countries. 3–4 hours per week (January 1904).
- P 361. Good version of Avigdor's "purpose and method" of the school in response to a graduate's letter about the reality of the school. "Between the dreams of the parents and reality…"
- P 362. GREAT letter from the student about the real condition of the school, from his view. The school exploits the students (!).
- P 378. Map of new parcel of land. Shows which parcels the Farm School owns.
- P 360. Bourgalo is looking to go anywhere—Brazil, America…
- P 441. 1903–1904 student placements or results. Jack Mitrani must have been part of the group going to Varna.
- P 444. Where students went in 1903–4. Mitrani went to Varna.
- P 470. November 1904 report on what the teachers were teaching and how many hours. It might give a good description of what the days were like.
- P 472. A paragraph about the students who went to Varna. Some of them are obviously leaving.
- P 478. Letter about the kids leaving Varna. Very blotchy and hard to read.
- P 480. Letter from the students in Varna describing their experience and why they were leaving. November 8, 1904.
- P 504. Strong letter from Avigdor about how badly the students were treated in Varna. Mentions mistreatment by Russian Jews.
- P 506. Letter from Safartti with good descriptions of the Varna students' situations
- P 529. More about Varna
- P 530. Letter from Avigdor to Sarfati (Director of Alliance School in Varna)

- P 535. Lists students going to Egypt. 3 out of 4 are from Adrinople
- P 552. Students get vacation from 6 Sept to 4 Oct
- P 558. About the Flour Mill lab
- P 563. Torrid heat 17 August
- P 573. Letter about the following article. Some minor details wrong, but it's a good article.
- PP 574–80. Transcription of article in Depeche Coloniale that describes the school
- P 611. Student (Amelar) going to NY. Passing up sharecropping opportunity. Avigdor says it should be at his own cost.
- PP 612–13. Letter from Amelar asking for help with the cost
- P 626. Two students decide not to go to Varna but go back to their original plan of going to Smyrna
- P 627–8. Letter from students mentioned above
- P 641. 44 degrees C in the shade, 111 F. 25 July 1904.
- PP 642–650. Lots of stuff about building the flour mill. Seems to be the major project.
- P 651. Avigdor supports Amelar's request. It seems that his parents were already in NY.
- PP 652–3. Another letter to Paris from Avigdor
- P 655. Letters from students in Varna
- P 658. Potential new students from Tunis. Includes Ben. Boccara's brother, Joseph. Avigdor doesn't recommend Bismuth even though his uncle wrote a letter reminding how much he supports the school.
- P 675. The Flour Mill is obviously a way to generate program revenue by exporting flour to Algeria and France.
- P 720. Fight between students. Lots of insults. June 29th, 1904. Sounds like a big deal if it had to be reported to Paris. But Avigdor was away. The report was written by Leven (sp?), his deputy.
- P 739. JCA Students willing to go to America
- P 753. The school's blacksmith quit

- P 761. Avigdor asks if the JCA can arrange for Mitrani and Romy to go to Canada. (Romy also could go to Egypt.) There is mention of Brasil. 1 June 1905.
- P 787. Map of Djédéida Farm with adjacent properties
- P 790. Visit from the vice president of the geographical society of Paris who said, "I would like to say I had the satisfaction of finding in Tunisia a practical agricultural school that couldn't be better organized and put together."
- P 804. Schedule and description of classes
- P 811. Bulgarian students don't find serious employment in Bulgaria and should go to Cyprus (?), Egypt, or Canada
- P 817. Avigdor writes about naturalizing the Tunisians and farm students as French citizens. Basically, it sounds like the Tunisian press is saying it's OK to naturalize individuals, but not groups. Citizenship again…
- P 818. Letter back from Paris: Mitrani is willing to go to Canada
- P 822. Romy going to either Egypt or Canada
- P 823. Certificate of completion/good conduct for Romy, from the school
- P 827. Gershom Magrisso is a sharecropper. Chart shows what he grew.
- P 829. Avigdor decides to send Mitrani to Canada. Either the Alliance or JCA should pay his way.
- P 830. Letter from Mitrani. He is home in Andrionople. He decides he will go to Canada since the Alliance won't be buying land in Bulgaria.
- P 861. Bulgarian students now get an agricultural military deferment. M. Danon arranged it with the Bulgarian govt. The school is officially recognized.
- PP 871–4. Printed history of the school from its start. Possibly from the Bulletin? Good summary.
- P 877. Avigdor made a 6,000 franc loan to a student secured by the mortgage of the father's orchard in Andrinople

- P 909. Avigdor asks the central committee to send 180 francs to his niece, Marie, who is an instructor in Andrinople and credit him
- P 947. Avigdor sends money to his brother in Andrionople
- P 949. References that he is disappointed the students have to leave Bulgaria for Cyprus or Canada
- P 956. Marauders broke into a house. They need a police post in town (?). Talks about security.
- P 992. Letter from Avigdor laying out the history of placing students at Varna and how their troubles have affected the students at the school. Also, how to make it right.
- P 994. Letter from T.R. Pickman saying that farming in Bulgaria isn't what the students were trained for. The Alliance needs to buy land and set up its own system of labor.
- P 996. Two students being sent to Egypt
- P 997. Letter from school director in Alexandria Egypt
- P 1036. Varna students Nathan and Mitrani ready to go to either Cyprus or Canada
- P 1051. 30 Jan 1905. More about Varna Students. M. Safarti wrote a letter suggesting the Alliance buy land in the area. Avigdor offers to go to Bulgaria, but it won't be until July 9 (I think).
- P 1053. Letter from Safarti about what he has found out. He relayed Avigdor's questions to the farm owners but hasn't gotten a response. He talks about the Alliance buying land in Varna.
- P 1078. 16 January 1905. Accounting letter. The school cost is 450 francs per student, annually (about $2,000 in 2020).

- JCA Archives, Montreal. This is where the letter from the agent in Winnipeg was found. You can search the collection online, but not much has been digitized.
    - https://www.cjhn.ca/en/list?q=topic%3a%22Jewish+Colonization+Association+(JCA)%22&p=1&ps=&sort=title_sort+asc

New York 1910

- US Census and family immigration documents are contained in the Youcha Sanden Family Tree, Ancestry.com, curated by Emily Youcha
  - https://www.ancestry.com/family-tree/tree/104098955/family/familyview?cfpid=430039989628

Monastir 1911

- Alliance Archives. See above. Hopefully, the documents from the former Yugoslavia will soon be available online through the AIU.
- Manaki Photos. See above
- Serbian Registry of the Jewish Community. National Archives, Bitola
  - Compiled in the 1930s, this registry lists everyone in the Jewish community, their addresses, occupations, and family members.
- Ancestry.com for immigration documents. See above
- Recording of tape with Vida and Morris
  - https://www.dropbox.com/s/m637uyyxw0b5g12/Morris%20and%20Vida%20Cassorla.mp3?dl=0
- *Report of the Carnegie International Commission to Inquire into the Causes and Conduct of the Balkan Wars*, Washington, DC, 1914
- List of Monastirlis who received clothes sent from community in NY through the JOINT after WWI
  - https://search.archives.jdc.org/multimedia/Documents/NY_AR1921/00024/NY_AR1921_00791.pdf#search=
- *The Bitola Jews*, Dimrovski, Bitola 1993
  - Page 116 talks about moneychangers
- 1929 Bitolan Jewish Almanac Report
  - *To the Statistics of the Jewry of the Kingdom of Serbs, Croats and Slovenes*
  - *K Statistici Jevrejstva Kraljevine S.H.S.*
  - In the fifth volume of the "Jewish Almanac" (1929)
  - https://jevrejskadigitalnabiblioteka.rs/handle/123456789/1704
  - https://jevrejskadigitalnabiblioteka.rs/bitstream/handle/123456789/1704/JAL5690KStatisticiJevrejstvaKraljevineSH-SOCR.pdf?sequence=1&isAllowed=y

New York 2020
- Susanna Weich-Shahak
  - Israeli National Library's Sound Archives, search for songs from Bitola.
    - https://merhav.nli.org.il/primo-explore/search?query =any,contains,Susana%20Weich-Shahak,%20bitola &tab=default_tab&search_scope=Local&vid=NLI &lang=iw_IL&offset=0
  - Songs from Monastir: Recordings of Simo and Alegre Calderon
    - https://www.nli.org.il/he/items/NNL_MUSIC_ AL002766279/NLI
- Cassorla/Elias Family Tree
  - http://cassorla.net/
- Avram Sadikario oral history
  - https://www.centropa.org/en/biography/avram-sadikario
  - Centropa is also a great resource for other Balkan Jew's oral histories, including Jamilla Kolonomos and Beno Ruso.
- Jamilla Kolonomos documented Jewish Macedonian history and proverbs
  - https://en.wikipedia.org/wiki/%C5%BDamila_Kolonomos
  - Jewish Digital Library: Downloadable pdf of her book of proverbs
    - https://core.ac.uk/outputs/336856916

New York 1920s–1930s
- Ancestry.com for immigration documents. See above
- Polk's Business Directory
  - New York Public Library
    - https://nypl.getarchive.net/media/polks-trows-new-york-city-directory-boroughs-of-manhattan-and-bronx-19331934-9d7020
- *A Study of the Monastir Dialect* by Max Luria

- Max Luria's field recordings. *Judeo-Spanish from the Balkans. The recordings of Julius Subak (1908) and Max A. Luria (1927), Series 12, Sound Documents from the Phonogrammarchiv of the Austrian Academy of Sciences, The Complete Historical Collections 1899–1950.*

Bitola 1920s–1930s
- *A Town Called Monastir*, Uri Oren
- Zionist Archive in Israel
  - http://www.zionistarchives.org.il/en/familyresearch/Pages/about-family-research.aspx
- Kamhi's report for the fifth volume of the "Jewish Almanac" (1929). See above
- Mark Cohen, *The Last Century*... See above

Bitola 1941–1943
- *Tide and Wreck: History of the Jews of Vardar Macedonia*/Jennie Lebel; translated from Serbian by Paul Münch. Excellent history of what the Bugarians did and how they used anti-Semitic taxes and laws.
- Mark Cohen, *The Last Century*...
- Jamilla Kolonomos' works and oral history. See above
- Avram Sadikario oral history. See above
- Beno Ruso oral history
  - https://www.centropa.org/en/biography/beno-ruso
- Jewish American newspapers about Rabbi Alcalay's escape
  - https://www.nli.org.il/en/newspapers/refadv/1942/07/31/01/article/25/?srpos=13&e=-------en-20--1--img-txIN%7ctxTI-%22Isaac+Alcalay%22-------------1
- Demitir Pechev, Yad Vashem biography
  - https://www.yadvashem.org/yv/en/exhibitions/righteous/peshev.asp
- Holocaust Memorial Center for Jews of Macedonia. This is the Holocaust Museum in Skopje.
  - http://www.holocaustfund.org/
- USHMM online exhibit about Monastir

- https://encyclopedia.ushmm.org/content/en/article/jewish-community-of-monastir-a-community-in-flux
- Yad Vashem online exhibit about Monastir
  - https://www.yadvashem.org/yv/en/exhibitions/communities/monastir/before20century.asp
- Steven Sage is writing a book on Bulgaria during the Holocaust. Not published, yet.
- Jacob Aroesti's Yizkor book link. There is a private translation into English.
  - https://digitalcollections.nypl.org/items/7bba8840-9950-0134-210d-00505686a51c/book#page/3/mode/2up

Bitola 2022
- North Macedonia National Archives
  - https://arhiv.mk/
- Albert Kahn Museum Interactive map of photos
  - https://opendata.hauts-de-seine.fr/explore/dataset/archives-de-la-planete/map/?disjunctive.operateur&location=9,41.26645,22.1347&basemap=jawg.streets
- Info about what is possibly Bochora's picture from 1913 in the Albert Kahn Museum
  - **Numéro d'inventaire,** A 2 062, **Opérateur,** Auguste Léon, **Légende d'origine,** Serbie, Monastir Bitolj, Femme israëlite, coiffure ducat, **Légende** Femme israëlite, coiffure en pièces d'or (dukati), **Lieu ancient** Monastir (actuelle Bitola), Macédoine, **Lieux** Bitola (Macédoine (FYROM)/Balkans/Europe), **Date de prise de vue** mai 1913, **Mission** Mission Jean Brunhes et Auguste Léon dans les Balkans au printemps 1913, **Sujets** Coiffure/couvre-chef, **Licence** Librement réutilisable (CC–00)—Domaine Public.
- Photo of Alliance Boy's School class taken in front of the Girl's School. AIU Digital Library.
  - https://www.bibliotheque-numerique-aiu.org/en/records/item/8553-eleves-et-professeurs-dans-la-cour?offset=1
- Six Petaled Flower

- How to draw
  - https://historicbuildinggeometry.uk/article/drawing-daisy-wheel-angles/
- Significance in Judaism
  - https://spadeandthegrave.com/2019/04/17/protect-the-grave-the-hexfoil-in-an-early-mortuary-context/

Six Petaled Flower

The six petaled flower design first appeared in my life when we visited the Bitolan cemetery in 2018. Carved into several gravestones in the cemetery, it now graces my oud and the cover of this book. In our 2022 trip to Bitola, Goce showed us a storage building marked with the Star of David and this flower. When Zack visited Hijar, he stood in the arch of the women's entrance to the synagogue. The flower is there, too.

Geometrically called a hexafoil, this basic "daisywheel" construction uses seven circles. Drawing it only requires some form of a drafting compass. Probably a carryover from pagan times, the figure serves as a protective symbol throughout Eastern Europe watching over buildings and graves. I even found it on the back of a 150-year-old Pennsylvania Dutch hammer dulcimer Dan Elias gave me from his father's basement collection.

In Judaism, the design can symbolize the flowers in the Bible and mean many things, such as renewal of life or protection of a home. It's also found on the sides of two-thousand-year-old ossuary boxes made to contain Jewish bones. This flower keeps coming up in my life. It obviously meant something to the Jews of Monastir. It still does. Zack is using it as a logo for his music project. Emma incorporated into a Challah cover written in Solitreo.

www.ingramcontent.com/pod-product-compliance
Lightning Source LLC
Chambersburg PA
CBHW051642230426
43669CB00013B/2409